Teaching Real-Life Writing to Young Learners

Easy Teacher-Tested Lessons That Help Children Learn to Write Lists, Letters, Invitations, How-Tos, and Much More

Paula Jensvold

New York • Toronto • London • Auckland • Sydney
Mexico City • New Delhi • Hong Kong • Buenos Aires

Teaching *Resources*

Acknowledgment

In appreciation to the many teachers who have crossed my path in the last ten years. You have all been an inspiration and taught me to love teaching and learning more and more with each year that passes.

Editor: Joan Novelli
Cover design and photograph: Maria Lilja
Interior design: Holly Grundon
Interior photographs: Paula Jensvold
Interior illustrations: Teresa Anderko, Maxie Chambliss, and James Graham Hale

ISBN-13: 978-0-545-15431-4
ISBN-10: 0-545-15431-6

Contents

Writing Lessons

Dear Reader and Writer,

At the beginning of each school year, I introduce my students to Writers' Workshop. They learn what a Writers' Workshop sounds like, looks like, and feels like. Each day, Writers' Workshop begins with a mini-lesson that targets a specific writing skill. The children then have an independent writing time and finally a share session at the end of the workshop. By the end of  September, anyone entering the classroom can observe children busy at tables and with clipboards, writing away, conferencing with teachers, and fully engaged in the writing process.

Children's first pieces of writing are "small-moment stories," or personal narratives about their lives. By around mid-October, after I have set the stage and launched Writers' Workshop, they need a change from writing these personal narratives. They need something different to rejuvenate and continue their interest in writing. They need to understand that writing for different purposes is part of their everyday lives. It was one sunny day in mid-October when I developed a unit of writing titled "Writing for Many Purposes." During this unit, children explore various real-life reasons for writing. They discover the different types of writing that they and their families already do in their daily lives—from making grocery lists to writing messages. This unit of writing also offers a wonderful way to integrate the content of writing with the mechanics of writing from the beginning, so that children see those skills as a natural part of what they do every day.

Through trial and error and the collaboration of many colleagues, that unit grew into the lessons that I share with you in this book. I invite you to try these lessons and make your own changes, and hope that they become a successful tool in your classroom for helping children become confident lifelong writers!

Happy writing!

Paula Jensvold

Teaching Real-Life Writing to Young Learners

About This Book

Young children learn best by experiencing their world, and that approach holds true for writing. When writing relates to real life, children naturally seem to be even more engaged. When children see family members making grocery lists, or their teachers writing the "morning message," they want to try the same thing—and become writers like the people around them. This book is in response to this need children have to experience meaningful reasons to write. *Teaching Real-Life Writing to Young Learners* is full of ideas for inviting children to write every day, and grow as confident and capable writers.

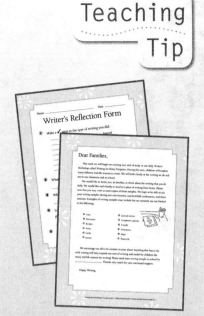

Pages 11–12 feature two reproducible templates you can use to enhance your writing unit. The first, a send-home letter (page 11), invites families to share examples of real-life writing they do at home with the class. You can adapt this letter as needed to fit your particular needs. A Writer's Reflection Form (page 12) provides a self-assessment tool that students can use whenever they write. You may want to place copies of this form at the Writing Center.

Why Teach So Many Different Types of Writing?

Teaching children to write for real purposes helps them see connections to their everyday lives. In *Units of Study for Primary Writing: A Yearlong Curriculum*, authors Lucy Calkins and Leah Mermelstein discuss the importance of helping children to realize that during every section of the day there are reasons to write. They note that teaching children the mastery of each genre is not the main focus, but rather teaching why we write shows children the purpose and encourages children to become lifelong writers. When children learn the purpose of writing, they learn to appreciate and enjoy writing. They no longer view writing as a chore but instead as a tool to better help explain their thinking.

When writing becomes a part of children's daily routine, they become fluent writers. In *Notebook Know-How: Strategies for the Writers' Notebook*, author Aimee Buckner stresses the importance of children being able to think and write at the same time. Getting words on a page quickly is an important skill for children to learn. When they write with ease and quickness, they become confident and learn to take risks. They learn to truly use writing as a part of their lives.

All teachers want the same thing for their children. We don't want to hear "I have nothing to write," or "I don't know what to do." What we do want is for children to feel energized by writing and to be encouraged each day that they have something important to say and that writing is one way to express themselves. We want all children to naturally view writing as a natural part of their day.

Teaching With the Lessons

This book is a collection of the lessons that I use with my students, and is designed to provide support for the various approaches to teaching writing that educators implement in their classrooms. Some teachers will find it helpful to use a lesson to introduce a strand of writing and then will move along to another lesson and strand. Other teachers will find that they want to further pursue a lesson with their students, and in this case will find the Follow-Up Mini-Lessons and Class Project provided for each main lesson helpful in elongating a strand of writing. A closer look at these and other lesson components follows.

Introduction
Each lesson begins with a "writing-in-action" photograph and a classroom anecdote that demonstrates how easy it is to make real-life writing connections in the classroom.

Writing Lesson
This section provides a sample script for teaching the lesson. Use the script as a guide for introducing and teaching the lesson, adapting the language, length, and level to meet the needs of your students. Each Writing Lesson concludes with suggestions for independent writing.

Follow-Up Mini-Lessons
Use some or all of the ideas in this section for further instruction with small groups and to provide additional opportunities for students to practice the particular form of writing.

Class Project
Take the writing topic further with an activity that engages students collaboratively in applying what they've learned. These fun projects range from creating school signs for Open House (page 45) to making a class "how-to" book (page 59), with each student contributing a set of directions for drawing something.

Literature Links
To support the reading-writing connection, each lesson includes a list of books that relate in some way to the particular strand of writing. These books serve as good read-alouds and as books that can be used to launch a mini-lesson around a type of writing.

Reproducible Pages
Ready-to-use templates make it easy to stock your classroom with inviting list forms, stationery, pop-up cards, postcards, and other materials that will inspire writing. Additional reproducible pages include related forms and activities.

More Real-Life Writing Lessons
Pages 88 through 96 feature suggestions for additional real-life writing lessons, including business cards (always a hit with children), recipes, e-mail, and more. You can use these ideas to launch mini-lessons or use them to develop more comprehensive writing lessons. These suggestions also make perfect Writing Center activities, providing students with playful reasons to practice writing every day.

Classroom Management Tips
Keep the following suggestions in mind as you plan your writing lessons. From noticing writing connections throughout the day to setting up writing folders, these practices will enrich your writing program and help children see themselves as writers.

1 Write Every Day
Have children write every day! Even if it is for a short amount of time, or together in a group, make time for a writing connection each day. Elementary classrooms are filled with possibilities such as a daily Morning Message, people to thank, celebrations, and family communications. You can always find a reason to write.

2 Take Time to Teach Routine

Take time in the beginning of the year to teach children the routine of writing. Teach them what a Writers' Workshop will look like and sound like. Teach them where they will keep their writing. Assign writing partners who can help if a teacher is busy.

3 Think of Yourself as a Writer

Take time to think of all the times in a day that you write. Demonstrate this to children by making a list with them. Show them examples of your own writing. Modeling good writing habits encourages children to become confident, lifelong writers.

4 Always Start With a Mini-Lesson

Always start a Writers' Workshop by teaching your students something new. It can be as easy as teaching children where to put their names on a sheet of paper or as sophisticated as teaching different ways to end a letter. But always teach them something!

It is important to organize and label writing materials. Baskets labeled with pictures and words let children efficiently find materials and put them back quickly. This organization keeps a Writers' Workshop running smoothly!

5 Create a Writing Center

Create a space in your classroom that makes materials easily accessible to students. Include all papers, coloring tools, writing tools, and supplies that they will need to become writers. Start out slowly, only putting out what you have taught children to use. Add in new materials to keep writing fresh! (For more on setting up a Writing Center, see page 9.)

6 Writing Folders

Have each child keep a writing folder. Keeping children's writing in a folder encourages them to revisit old pieces. Having their writing folders handy is a great way to wrap up at the end of a Writers' Workshop. Keeping writing in folders makes it easy for children to share and spread out work when it comes time to choose a piece to publish.

7 Sharing Circle

Always end Writers' Workshop with a sharing circle. A sharing circle is a great way to reflect on the day's writing or even teach something new. Children learn best from listening to other children's writing. Even though it takes extra minutes in your day, don't forget to meet in a circle and wrap up!

In order to be writers, children need access to different types of paper, stamps, stencils, and coloring utensils that match the type of writing that they want to do for a specific purpose. A Writing Center is a great place to store all of these materials. Consider the location of the Writing Center carefully, if possible placing it near storage shelves (for paper and other supplies) as well as where there is wall space to display helpful wall charts (such as a "friendly letter" template with parts labeled) and examples of writing work.

Shelves with easy-to-access bins encourage independence.

Begin building your Writing Center slowly, offering just one or two types of paper and writing tools that your students already know how to use. As you teach new writing lessons, add materials to the center that are appropriate for that lesson. For example, after teaching a lesson on writing postcards (see page 20), it makes sense to add postcard templates and stamp pads to the center. Adding materials slowly is important because children need to know and learn how to use the materials. This will help ensure the proper use of materials as well as keep them organized.

The list of suggested materials that follows is based on the writing lessons provided in this book. Modify the list as needed to best support your writing program.

Art Supplies

Colored pencils
Crayons
"Dot" markers
Glitter pens
Ink pads and stamps
Markers
Pencils
Scissors
Stencils
Tape

Writing Paper Templates

Lists (pages 18–19)
Postcards (pages 24–25)
Cards (pages 30–32)
Letters (page 38)
Surveys (pages 46 and 96)
Signs (page 47)
Messages (page 52)
How-To Directions (page 60)
Journals (page 65)
Ads (page 70)
Invitations (pages 75–76)
Maps (pages 81–82)
Stories (pages 87)
E-mail (page 94)
Book Review (page 95)

Other Materials

Basket of books about writing
Basket of books that represent different forms of writing (see Literature Links for each lesson)
Class mailbox
Paper clips
Plastic organizer with drawers (for storing small items, such as paper clips)
Stamps (for letters and postcards; see page 22)
Stapler
Telephone
Writing folders (and bin for storage)
Writer's Reflection Form (page 12)

Meeting the Standards

The lessons and activities in this book support the following standards for students in grades K–2, outlined by Mid-continent Research for Education and Learning (McREL), an organization that collects and synthesizes national and state PreK–12 curriculum standards.

Uses the general skills and strategies of the writing process:

* Uses prewriting strategies to plan written work (discusses ideas with peers)

* Uses strategies to draft written work (adds descriptive words)

* Uses strategies to edit and publish written work (incorporates illustrations)

* Evaluates own and others' writing

* Uses strategies to organize written work

* Uses writing and other methods to describe familiar persons, places, objects, or experiences

* Writes in a variety of forms or genres

* Writes for different purposes (to entertain, inform, learn, communicate ideas)

Uses the stylistic and rhetorical aspects of writing:

* Uses descriptive words to convey basic ideas

Uses grammatical and mechanical conventions in written compositions:

* Uses complete sentences in written compositions

* Uses nouns in written compositions (nouns for simple objects, family members, community workers, and categories)

* Uses verbs in written compositions (verbs for a variety of situations, action words)

* Uses adjectives in written compositions (uses descriptive words)

* Uses adverbs in written compositions (uses words that answer how, when, where, and why questions)

References and Resources

Buckner, A. (2005). *Notebook know-how: Strategies for the writers' notebook*. Portland, ME: Stenhouse.

Calkins, L., & Mermelstein, L. (2003). *Units of study for primary writing: A yearlong curriculum*. Portsmouth, NH: Heinemann.

Duke, N. K., & Bennett-Armistead, V. S. (2003). *Reading & writing informational text in the primary grades: Research-based practices*. New York: Scholastic.

Kendall, J. S., & Marzano, R. J. (2004). *Content knowledge: A compendium of standards and benchmarks for K–12 education*. Aurora, CO: Mid-continent Research for Education and Learning. Online database: http://www.mcrel.org/standards-benchmarks.

Miller, D. (2002). *Reading with meaning*. Portland, ME: Stenhouse.

Rothstein, G. (1999). *Real-life writing activities based on favorite picture books*. New York: Scholastic.

Dear Families,

This week we will begin an exciting new unit of study in our daily Writers' Workshop called Writing for Many Purposes. During this unit, children will explore many different real-life reasons to write. We will look closely at the writing we do and see in our classroom and in school.

We would like to invite you, as families, to think about the writing that you do daily. We would like each family to send in a piece of writing from home. Please note that you may wish to send copies of these samples. We hope to be able to use your writing samples during our mini-lessons, teacher/child conferences, and share sessions. Examples of writing samples may include but are certainly are not limited to the following:

❈ Lists	❈ Journal entries
❈ Directions	❈ Scrapbook captions
❈ Recipes	❈ E-mails
❈ Notes	❈ Invitations
❈ Cards	❈ Maps
❈ Letters	❈ Postcards

We encourage you all to be creative in your ideas! Anything that has to do with writing will help expand our unit of writing and model for children the many real-life reasons for writing! Please send your writing sample to school by _____. Thanks very much for your continued support.

Happy Writing,

Name: _____   Date: _____

Writer's Reflection Form

1   Make a ✔ next to the type of writing you did:

_____ List	_____ Journal
_____ Postcard	_____ Advertisement
_____ Card	_____ Invitation
_____ Letter	_____ Map
_____ Sign	_____ Small-Moment Story
_____ Telephone Message	_____ Other:
_____ Directions	_____

2   What I like best about my piece of writing: _____

_____

3   What I would improve next time: _____

_____

4   Something I learned about writing while I worked on this

piece: _____

_____

5   Color the stars to show how you did.

Lesson 1

Creating Lists

"I can't believe that I forgot my homework again this week!"

If I had a penny for every time that I heard this from my students! It is Friday, the day I collect homework folders, and four children have forgotten to bring their folders to school. It is a perfect day for a lesson on creating lists. Your early writers, as well as English-language learners, will find making lists an easier task than jumping right into a story, making this a great first writing lesson.

Introducing the Lesson

Writing lists is a simple and doable task for all elementary children, no matter what level writers they are. Children easily relate to this real-life form of writing and see many uses for list-writing in their everyday lives. Families create grocery lists and to-do lists, even lists as they prepare for a trip. Lists are also a familiar form of writing for many children as birthdays and holidays draw near. Writing lists is the perfect way to get children excited about writing. It fits into everyone's life and is a skill that helps build responsibility.

Adapt the sample dialogue that follows, which is based on writing-lesson conversations in my classroom, to introduce and teach this purpose for writing.

Teacher: *Girls and boys, today I noticed that lots of children forgot their homework folders. Has this ever happened to you before?*

Student: *Yes. It's so hard to remember my homework folder when I am trying to remember my library books, snow pants, mittens, hat, and lunch.*

Teacher: *You are right! This time of year it is hard to remember everything. Today I will share a new writing trick with you. When I have a lot of things to remember for school, for example, when we are doing a special project, I sit down the night before and make a list of everything that I need to bring to school so I don't forget anything in the morning. Let me show you what I mean.*

Next week is Valentine's Day. In our classroom we always celebrate with a pancake breakfast. There are lots of things that I need to bring to school to feed you all pancakes. Talk with your writing partner about things that I might need to bring in order to have a pancake breakfast for our class.

[Give children plenty of time to share ideas with their partners.]

Teacher: *I heard lots of great ideas. Is anyone ready to share?*

Student: *You will need to bring pancake mix, eggs, and milk. That's what my mom uses to make pancakes.*

Student: *You also need to bring something to cook the pancakes on, like a griddle.*

Student: *How about plates? And forks.*

Student: *I like maple syrup.*

[Children will have lots of ideas. Continue accepting suggestions until you feel you have enough for a complete list.]

Teacher: *Wow! Can you see how easy it would be to forget something? Watch as I write down some of your ideas.* [List on chart paper or the board.] *I will start with a title: Valentine's Day Breakfast. Then I will write your ideas beneath that. I will write one idea on each line.*

Valentine's
Day Breakfast

Pancake mix
Eggs
Milk
Griddle
Maple syrup
Plates
Forks
Measuring Cups
Mixing Bowl
Mixing Spoon
Spatula
Cups
Fruit
Juice

Teaching Real-Life Writing to Young Learners

Teacher: *This is perfect. Now, on the morning of Valentine's Day, I can take out this list and check off each item as I pack up everything in a bag. This way, I won't forget anything!*

People make lists so that they don't forget important things. Your families might make lists when they go grocery shopping or get ready to take a trip. People also make to-do lists of things they need to take care of, like returning library books and going to the bank. Sometimes people make to-do lists of chores they need to accomplish at home or at work. My to-do list this week reminds me that I need to pay the bills and clean the closet. Kids can make lists of things they need to remember, too. They can make a list of things they need to bring to school or soccer practice. You'll see lists in our classroom, too. Take a look around. What are some lists you see?

[Allow time for children to point out and discuss lists on the classroom walls, such as attendance lists, school lunch lists, and supply lists.]

Teacher: *Today, we're going to make some lists. You'll see that I added new "list" paper in our Writing Center. I have also added some list paper with titles. If you are stuck for an idea, try using one of those list papers to get started. Happy writing!*

[Share a sample of each reproducible List Template (pages 18–19) with students. Model how to add a title to the blank list paper. Review choices for the list papers that already have titles. See also Teaching Tip, page 16.]

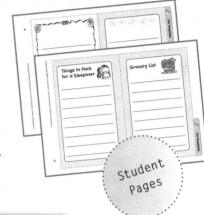

Student Pages

Follow-Up Mini-Lessons

To do more with list-writing, try these mini-lessons. They're perfect for use during a Writers' Workshop, as a choice-time activity, or with small groups for further instruction.

Categorize Vocabulary
Tie in a lesson about categorizing and grouping like objects. Give children a group of words (such as ocean words) and have them sort the words into different categories or groups such as animals and plants. Have them list each word in the correct group.

Gather Story Ideas
Have students use journals to gather lists of ideas for stories. You might provide prompts for students to respond to:

❖ List five things that make you feel happy

❖ List five activities that you like to do after school

❖ List five things that happened to you yesterday

❖ List five words that you think of when I say "green"

Encourage children to review their lists when they need inspiration for a writing topic.

Practice Alphabetical Order

When children start to create lists, it is a great time to introduce the concept of alphabetical order, a characteristic of many lists children will encounter. Have children alphabetize their spelling words using word cards and an alphabet strip. As children become more and more independent with alphabetizing words, challenge them to arrange themselves in alphabetical order when lining up to go to lunch or as a Morning Meeting game.

Explore an Index

Introduce the term *index* in nonfiction text as a list of words located at the back of a book that helps you quickly find important information without reading every page of a book. Guide students in discovering how the list is arranged (in alphabetical order). Use a nonfiction text with an index to set up a scavenger hunt. Have students take turns using the index to locate information about different topics.

Teaching Tip

Stock the dramatic-play area of your classroom with list pads like the ones children's families might use at home. Make multiple copies of the List Templates (pages 18–19). Cut apart the list paper on the dashed lines. Use a large alligator clip to bind at the top. Place in the dramatic-play center for children to use in their activities.

Literature Links

The following titles introduce a number of real-life reasons to make lists.

Alexander Who Used to Be Rich Last Sunday by Judith Viorst (Atheneum, 1978): Alexander's grandma and grandpa come to visit and give Alexander and his two brothers each one dollar. There are many things to buy: bus tokens, snakes, and bets to have with his brothers, all of which he loses!

Freckle Juice by Judy Blume (Random House Children's Books, 1978): If children are familiar with this book, they will quickly note that Sharon, an unkind classmate, creates a pretend recipe to help Andrew get freckles.

Frog and Toad Together by Arnold Lobel (HarperCollins Publishers, 2008): Toad makes a very important list of things to do "today," crossing off each item as he does it. This favorite story gives children a realistic, easy-to-read example of a list.

Nate the Great and the Lost List by Marjorie Weinman Sharmat (Bantam Doubleday Dell, 1975): Claude's grocery list is missing. Even though Nate the Great is on vacation, he sets out to find it before lunch!

Teaching Real-Life Writing to Young Learners

Class Project: Things to Know

It is always a challenge to have a guest or substitute teacher in the classroom when you are out of the building. A useful class project, then, is to involve your students in helping to create a "Things to Know About Room ____" book. Follow these easy steps to ensure a helpful and creative book.

1. Brainstorm important information a guest teacher should know to help make sure that everyone has a good day. Use a class schedule to guide this discussion. List ideas on chart paper. Suggested topics include:

   ❋ Class list of names

   ❋ List of favorite greetings

   ❋ Schedule for each day of the week

   ❋ List of jobs

   ❋ List of meeting rules

   ❋ List of favorite recess activities

   ❋ List of favorite ways to practice spelling words

   ❋ List of favorite quick games (transitions)

   ❋ List of favorite songs

   ❋ List of favorite snacks

   ❋ List of things to do to get ready for dismissal

Student Work

2. Pair children and have partners choose one item from the list. Provide students with list paper (page 18), and have them go to work creating their lists. They can add illustrations if desired, or use different-colored pencils or pens to add color to their lists. Children might like to make a draft of their lists first, then rewrite them for inclusion in the book.

Grocery List

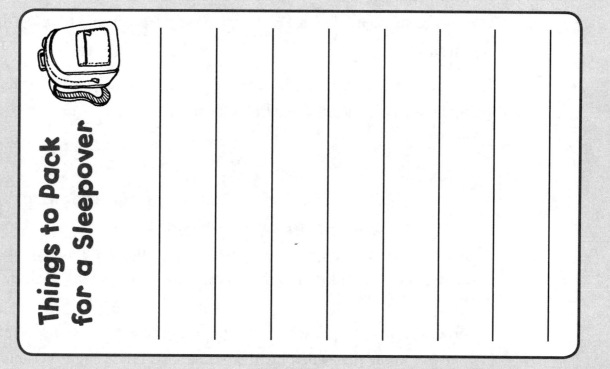

Things to Pack for a Sleepover

Sending Postcards

"Mrs. Jensvold, Mrs. Jensvold! My dad is in China for work and he sent me a postcard! Want to see?"

"Wow! What a beautiful picture. I have never been to China before. Now I know exactly what it looks like. What did your dad say on the back of the postcard?"

"He said that he misses me and someday he wants to take me to China with him. He also said that the food is yummy!"

Postcards are a great way to start getting your students to think about sending correspondence in the mail to a friend or loved one. Due to the fact that postcards are short, they are a manageable way for younger children to send a message. They are fast and fun and children often get an immediate sense of accomplishment in knowing that their piece of writing is being sent on, in the real mail system! I know that when I gather students on the rug for Writers' Workshop, they will all be eager to try writing a postcard.

Begin this lesson by discussing reasons people write postcards; sometimes they just want to send someone a short message, making them a perfect choice for those times you don't have a lot to say! Let children chime in with stories about postcards they've sent or received to reinforce the different reasons people send postcards, including as a way to say "hi" to someone special during a trip.

Adapt the sample dialogue that follows, which is based on writing-lesson conversations in my classroom, to introduce and teach this purpose for writing.

Teacher: *Girls and boys, I have noticed that many of you like to write letters. But sometimes you start writing and you don't have a lot to say. When you want to send someone special a short message, it sometimes works better if you send a postcard rather than a letter.*

Student: *I got a postcard once from my grandma when she was in Florida.*

Student: *Me too! My dad just sent me a postcard from China because he was away for work.*

Teacher: *That's right! Sometimes people send postcards when they are traveling. Other times people use postcards to send a short note or make an announcement. There are lots of ways to use postcards. Today we'll be using them to write a short message.*

Student: *Can I send one to my mom?*

Teacher: *Yes! You will all get to work on at least one postcard today that you will send to someone special. Before we get started, I think we better take a close look at the book* Arthur Goes to Camp. *This book is about Arthur going to camp. Instead of having a good time at camp, he is unhappy. See if you can figure out what Arthur is unhappy about by listening as I read aloud the postcards he sends.*

[Read *Arthur Goes to Camp* (Little, Brown, 1984), pausing to point out the postcards that Arthur has written. Have children turn to a partner and talk about what they see in each postcard. Ask: *Did Arthur write a lot or just a few sentences? What do you think is on the front of the postcard? How did he start his message? How did he end his message?*]

Teacher: *You noticed a lot in Arthur's postcards. Today you will all write a postcard to send to someone special you know. Arthur's postcard was being sent from camp, so his message was about camp. Your postcard is being sent from school, so your message will be about school. Turn to a friend and share three things that you might write about school.*

Teaching Tip

Student Pages

In advance of the lesson, make copies of each Postcard Template (pages 24–25). Be sure to have children's home addresses handy so that while they are working, you can go around and write each child's address as needed. Students might also consider "sending" their postcards to someone special at school, such as a former teacher, a cafeteria worker, or the principal.

[Allow time for students to share ideas about writing postcards.]

I heard lots of great things. I heard some of you say that you would tell your families we are learning about caterpillars and butterflies. I heard other kids talking about the class Estimation Jar. Those are two good examples of things to write about. If you get stuck for an idea, use our daily schedule to help you think about our day and the important things that we do each day.

[Give each student a Postcard Template. (See pages 24-25.) Demonstrate how to cut, fold, and glue the postcard. Then model how to complete each postcard. Begin by designing the front of the postcard and drawing a picture. Then show students how to turn over the postcard and write a message. As students complete their postcards, help them address the postcards for mailing.]

Invite families or the Parent Teacher Organization to donate stamps (letter and postcard) to keep in your writing center. As a class, write a letter explaining the request. This is a great way to introduce writing thank-you cards, too! (See Creating Cards, page 26.) Teach children the difference between the cost of a stamp for a letter and a postcard and the correct way to place the stamp on an envelope and postcard.

Follow-Up Mini-Lessons

Try some of these follow-up lessons to extend the lesson and provide focus with specific skills and concepts.

We've Got Mail Add a real mailbox to your Writing Center. Decorate the mailbox and add the room number. Demonstrate how the red flag works. Assign a student each day to take the mail down to the school's mailbox or "out-box." Create a space in the classroom where children can receive mail.

Left and Right Children often need reminders about where to start and stop writing on a postcard. Teach a mini-lesson that reinforces this skill, letting children use blank postcard templates to practice writing on the left side and leaving room for the address on the right.

Greetings and Salutations Brainstorm with students different greetings and closings. Make a wall chart of these ideas and display in the Writing Center for children to reference when writing.

Map It! Have families collect and send in postcards they receive from different places. Display the postcards on a map to integrate with the social studies curriculum and to provide inspiration for children when they are creating their own postcards.

Field Trip A field trip provides a perfect real-life reason to write. When returning from a field trip, give each child a blank postcard to fill out. Children can send the postcards to family members. These postcards provide children with a real-life writing connection, and families will love receiving something in the mail from their children.

Literature Links

Inspire postcard-writing in the classroom by sharing these fiction and nonfiction titles.

Arthur Goes to Camp by Marc Brown (Little Brown, 1984): Arthur is not happy about being at camp! Between poison ivy, rotten food, and unkind camp counselors, Arthur is ready to go home. Throughout his camp experience he writes postcards to let his family know just how unhappy he is—that, is until he wins a scavenger hunt!

Australia by Helen Arnold (Steck Vaughn, 1995): Postcards written by children offer an innovative approach to this nonfiction text about the cities, outback, coral reef, and other information about Australia.

Postcards From Pluto: A Tour of the Solar System by Loreen Leedy (Holiday House, 2006): Dr. Quasar gives a tour of the solar system from Mercury to Pluto, with informative postcards throughout. Symbols take the place of text on many of the postcards, which is a fun writing style children can try on their own!

Stringbean's Trip to the Shining Sea by Vera B. Williams and Jennifer Williams (William Morrow, 1988): Stringbean Coe, his brother Fred, and their dog Potato are driving across the country. Family members back home feel like they are part of the trip when the brothers send a postcard each day.

Class Project: Greetings From Room _____

Children love making their own stationery, including these special class postcards. Children can use the class postcards to write thank-you notes, announcements, and invitations that are going out from the whole class.

1. Across a sheet of 8 ½- by 11-inch drawing paper, write "Greetings From Room _____."

2. In the spaces around the greeting, have each child draw a self-portrait. Children can use pencil first, then trace over with a thin-lined back marker and sign their names. Remind children that everyone's picture is going on one sheet of paper.

3. Reduce the final piece of art by approximately 50 percent to create a postcard-sized image. Photocopy the postcard on card stock and keep a supply at the Writing Center.

Teaching Tip

Make a second version of the class postcard, this one with students' portraits only (no text). A set of these makes a lovely gift for class volunteers.

Postcard Template

Directions: Fold at the center line. Glue the backs together.

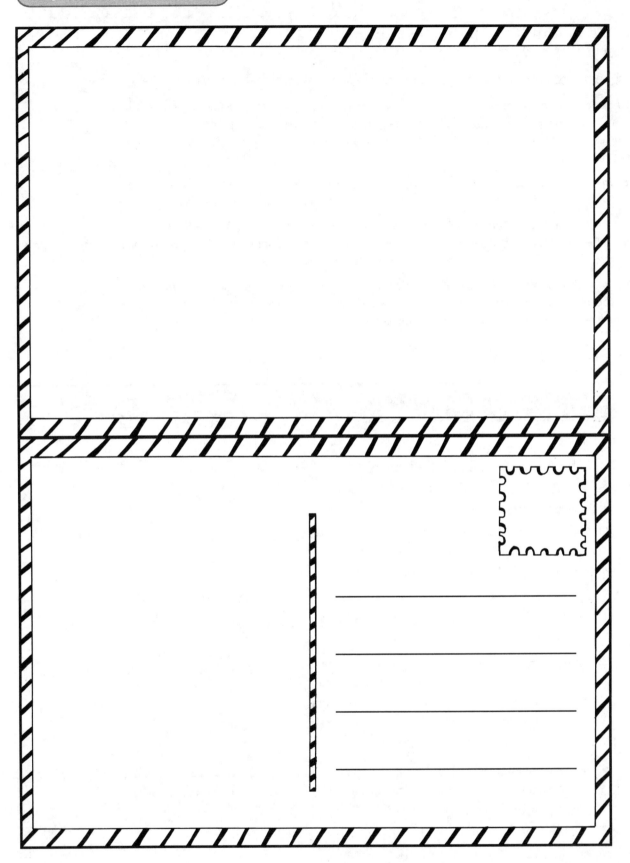

 Teaching Real-Life Writing to Young Learners © 2010 by Paula Jensvold. Scholastic Teaching Resources

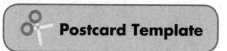

Directions: Fold at the center line. Glue the backs together.

Greetings From
_____

Postcard

Place
Stamp
Here

_____

_____

_____

_____

Creating Cards

"Good morning. Today is Tuesday, October 16.
Our lunch menu today is cheese or pepperoni pizza,
peanut butter and jelly, or tuna boat with veggie sticks.
Birthdays today are Mrs. Smith…"

Once I heard the announcements and found out that it was Mrs. Smith's birthday, I knew right away what my lesson in Writers' Workshop would be. A birthday in a classroom is a perfect opportunity to introduce making cards. It is also a wonderful time to talk about the difference between a card and a letter.

Introducing the Lesson

Card-making is an easy, fun, creative way to let children tell friends and loved ones how much they care about them. Teaching children to create cards can be as easy or complex as your time allows. Children seem to get the concept and can become successful card-makers in as little as a day. They also become quite skilled at spelling high frequency words, leaving correct spaces, and formulating witty sayings if given extra mini-lessons (see page 28) and time to explore ready-made cards.

Adapt the sample dialogue that follows, which is based on writing-lesson conversations in my classroom, to introduce and teach this purpose for writing.

Teacher: *Did you all listen carefully today during our morning announcements? I hope that you all heard the birthday announcements because we have a very special birthday to celebrate today—Mrs. Smith's!*

One way to help a person celebrate a birthday is to make a greeting card. A greeting card usually sends a short, special message to someone. Can anyone remember a time when you received a special card from someone?

Student: *I got a Halloween card in the mail from my grandma. It had stickers inside!*

Student: *I got a birthday card from my cousin.*

Teacher: *Think back to a time when you received a card, or perhaps your family received a card. Try to remember one thing that made the card special and interesting to read and look at. Talk to a person nearby to share your ideas.*

[Allow time for students to discuss their ideas.]

Can anyone tell me one thing you or your partner can remember about your special cards?

Student: *The cards that I usually get are very colorful and sometimes they have glitter on them!*

Student: *I got a card once that had a funny joke inside.*

Teacher: *You're right. Many greeting cards are fun to look at. Pictures and different colors make them interesting to look at and enjoy. Sometimes the pictures go with a special event, such as a birthday. So a birthday card might have a cake on it, or presents. Usually a card has very little writing on the outside and a few sentences on the inside. Sometimes even a joke! You watch as I begin to make Mrs. Smith a special birthday card. First, I need to think about folding a sheet of paper the correct way. I will fold my paper so Mrs. Smith can open the card like a book. You might even want to keep a book nearby to remind you before you start decorating or writing your card.*

> ## Teaching Tip
>
> People often have leftover stationery stored away in closets or boxes. Ask families and school staff to donate any unwanted stationery to your classroom. Children can use the stationery as is or turn it into cards.

Let's see, now that my paper is folded, I need to think about the outside of my card. It's her birthday so I will want to say something about a birthday. How about "Happy Birthday to You!" Then I'm going to draw a birthday cake with candles and add some balloons. Now, let's see what I should write inside. It should be a short message. Turn to a neighbor and talk about what you think I should write for a birthday message.

[Allow time for students to share their ideas.]

You all thought of wonderful ideas! I heard children saying that I could even write the "Happy Birthday" song.

[Model for students how to write a message on the inside of the card. This is a good time to discuss greetings and closings.]

Teacher: *At the Writing Center today, you'll find some special supplies for making birthday cards. Have fun making your cards. And remember that any day that you are writing, you might want to think about making a card for a special occasion.*

[Model for students how to cut out and fold the reproducible card templates (pages 30–32). For the Pop-Up Card Template (page 32), show students how to cut on the center lines, push the tab forward (to the inside of the card), and glue a picture to the tab (which becomes the "pop-up"). See sample at right.]

Follow-Up Mini-Lessons

Children love making cards. The suggestions here build on that interest to extend the lesson and enhance students' writing skills in general.

Special Occasion Wall Chart Make a list of special occasions when people send cards—for example, birthdays, various holidays, and births. Display the list for children to use as a spelling reference as well as an idea resource.

Bubble Letters Children love to make bubble letters! Take time to teach them how to make bubble letters so that you are not spending your conferencing time teaching each child or they are not wasting lots of paper with eraser marks. Here's one easy way: Use pencil to write a letter. Outline the letter using rounded edges. Erase the first single-line letter, then color in the shape. To make a bigger bubble letter, just outline the letter more than once. Then erase everything inside the final outline.

Get Creative With Lettering Introduce stencil letters to your Writing Center. Children will love to use stencils to give their cards a "professionally printed" look!

Uppercase or Lowercase? Children often confuse when to use uppercase and lowercase letters. Collect old greeting cards and invite children to examine the cards to look for uppercase and lowercase letters. Discuss when to use each form.

Literature Links

Children need to see lots of real-life circumstances for making cards. They need to see examples and read the language that cards are written in. Use these titles to give students lots of fun stories to go along with a lesson on creating cards.

Lottie's New Beach Towel by Petra Mathers (Atheneum, 1998): Lottie loves her new beach towel from her Aunt Mattie. It comes just in time to help Lottie solve problem after problem at the beach. Her clever thank-you note at the end of the story is a great way to encourage children to make and send a thank-you to someone special.

Nate the Great and the Mushy Valentine by Marjorie Weinman Sharmat (Random House, 1995): When Nate the Great finds a bright red heart-shaped Valentine taped to Sludge's doghouse, he must help his dog figure out the secret admirer's identity. Children will love the mystery as well as looking closely at the note for clues. This is a perfect book to use before Valentine's Day to get children thinking about making their own Valentine cards.

Thank You, Mr. Falker by Patricia Polacco (Penguin, 1998): The author shares the story of her childhood struggle with reading, and of the teacher who changed everything for her. This moving story may inspire children to write thank-you cards to people they appreciate.

Class Project: Happy Birthday to You

Children love saying "Happy Birthday" to staff members at school. This project lets them say "Happy Birthday" in their writing by creating cards they'll look forward to delivering throughout the year.

Student Work

1. Provide a few writing sessions for children to make birthday cards for staff members. (Each student makes a card for a particular staff member.) Collect the cards and store them in a basket in your meeting area along with the list of dates.

2. When a staff member's birthday is mentioned during the morning announcements, have a student find and deliver the card. If your school doesn't have regular announcements, add the staff names to your monthly calendar. Spending a few days on this project will enable you to fit in a few of the mini-lessons (page 28) to ensure successful card-making!

Fold Here

Happy Birthday!

✂ **Card Template**

Fold Here

Thank You!

Writing Letters

Good morning,

*Today is March 18. We got mail! Meet me on the rug and be
ready to open our mail after the morning announcements.*

Love,

Mrs. Jensvold

After reading the day's morning message, my students are quick to get to
the rug for our meeting. They're eager to open our class envelope. They
want to know right away who sent them something in the mail. I explain that
by looking in the top left corner, we can see the name of the person and their
address. They see right away that it is from a former teacher who moved away,
Mrs. Bruns. We read the letter several times and learn that Mrs. Bruns is very
happy in her new home. Her two children love their new school and have even
been on a field trip to the ocean! Mrs. Bruns has a few questions for us that we
will need to write back and answer, creating a perfect opportunity to teach the
form of a friendly letter.

Letter-writing is a lost art in many households. With so many different means of communication, such as e-mail, cell phones, and text messages, children do not often have the opportunity to sit down and write a letter. I am often surprised that when I ask children if anyone has ever received a letter in the mail, only a few hands go up! Families still spend the time to send greeting cards, but very few letters are sent through the mail. This lesson gives all the children an opportunity to write a letter.

Adapt the sample dialogue that follows, which is based on writing-lesson conversations in my classroom, to introduce and teach this purpose for writing.

Teaching Tip

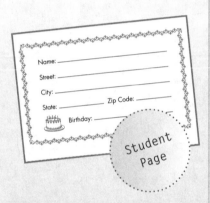

Name: _____
Street: _____
City: _____
State: _____ Zip Code: _____
Birthday: _____

Student Page

Children's lives are filled with special people. Use the reproducible Address Book Template (page 39) to create mini address books. Send home an address book with each child and encourage parents to fill in names and addresses of people to whom their children would like to write throughout the year. Don't forget to have them add each person's birthday so children can send birthday cards if they like.

Teacher: *It was very exciting this morning to get a letter in the mail from Mrs. Bruns. A letter is different from a card. Today we are going to learn about writing letters. First, we need to think about what goes in a letter. Let's take a close look at the letter from Mrs. Bruns. How does her letter begin?*

Student: *It says, "Dear Mrs. Jensvold's Class."*

Teacher: *That's right. Letters usually begin with the word* dear*. This part of the letter is called the "greeting." What comes next?*

Student: *There's a lot of stuff! She told us about the field trip she took with her children.*

Student: *And about her new house.*

Teacher: *The part of the letter with "lots of stuff" is called the* body*. And you are right! It does tell "lots of stuff." People often write letters to tell about something. They might even be writing to ask questions.*

Student: *Mrs. Bruns did that! She wanted to know when our end-of-the-year play was going to be. She also wanted to know what our play will be about.*

Teacher: *How does the letter end?*

Student: *At the end, it says, "Love, Mrs. Bruns."*

Teacher: *That's right. The end part of a letter is called the* closing*. I think Mrs. Bruns chose the word* love *because she knows us really well. If you didn't know the person well, you might use the word* sincerely *or* from*.*

Teacher: *If we were to write a letter back to Mrs. Bruns, I think we would start with "Dear Mrs. Bruns." That's the easy part. The most important part is what we will choose to write in the body of the letter. Turn and talk with a partner. If you were going to write back to Mrs. Bruns, what would you be sure to put in your letter? What questions might you ask her?*

[Allow time for students to share ideas about writing to someone. Offer prompts as needed, such as "What is something interesting that is happening in our classroom?"]

Teacher: *I heard many great ideas! I heard a few of you say that you would tell Mrs. Bruns about the birds we are studying in Science Workshop. I also heard someone say that Mrs. Bruns might like to hear about the gymnastics you're doing in P.E. Did anyone think of a question to ask Mrs. Bruns?*

Student: *I did! I want to know what her new job is.*

Student: *I want to know if she has nice neighbors at her new house.*

Teacher: *Those are both good questions. Today we're going to write back to Mrs. Bruns. Think about her letter to us, and remember to answer the questions that she asked us in her letter, and to tell her about a few things. You can also ask her some questions.*

Student Page

[Provide assorted stationery for letter-writing, such as the reproducible paper on page 38.]

Follow-Up Mini-Lessons

From comparing and contrasting different types of correspondence (such as cards, letters, and postcards) to teaching basic skills such as spacing and capitalization, there are lots of ways to extend a letter-writing lesson. The following ideas will help turn your first lesson on letter-writing into days of writing and learning!

Alike and Different
Children often have a difficult time telling the difference between greeting cards and letters. They often choose to write a letter but only say "Happy Birthday" or "I miss you." Create a mini-lesson that compares the differences and similarities between cards and letters. A Venn diagram is a good way to approach this.

Word-Wall Words Create a Word Wall of words that are often used in letters, including *Dear, Sincerely, Love,* and *Your friend.* Have children practice writing these words on personal dry-erase boards. Discuss rules for capitalizing words in salutations and closings.

Spacing Spend some time focusing on correct spacing in a letter. Where does the greeting go? What happens if children don't use all of the lines? Does their closing still go at the bottom? You might write parts of a simple friendly letter on sentence strips and let children arrange them in order on a pocket chart.

Stamp It Once children have mastered letter-writing, have them practice writing the school's return address on the envelope. You can also use a school address stamp and teach children to leave room to write their name at the top.

Literature Links

There are many wonderful children's books in which letter-writing helps tell the story. Whether the letters in these books are familiar, funny, or heartwarming, they are sure to inspire lots of letter-writing in the classroom.

Dear Mr. Blueberry by Simon James (Simon & Schuster, 1996): During summer vacation, Emily spots a whale in her backyard pond, and writes a letter to her dear teacher Mr. Blueberry. Mr. Blueberry writes back to tell her she must be mistaken, and a summer of correspondence begins.

Dear Mrs. LaRue: Letters From Obedience School by Mark Teague (Scholastic, 2002): Ike is a cat-chasing dog whose aggravated owner finally packs him off to obedience school, where he commences a letter-writing campaign detailing the horrors of his experience.

Flat Stanley by Jeff Brown (HarperCollins, 2003): This wonderful read-aloud will have children wondering what would happen if a bulletin board landed on them and made them flat. They could be mailed away to a different state in an envelope, fly as a kite, or even fit into a drain!

I Wanna Iguana by Karen Kaufman Orloff (Penguin Group, 2004): Alex desperately wants an iguana. Through a series of notes to his mother, he promises to take good care of the iguana, as well as show her that he knows all there is to know about iguanas.

The Jolly Postman: Or Other People's Letters by Janet and Allan Ahlberg (Little Brown, 2001): The pages of this delightful story include real envelopes and letters written from one fairy-tale character to another.

With Love, Little Red Hen by Alma Flor Ada (Simon & Schuster, 2004): Through a series of charming letters they write to one another, Little Red Hen and other fairy-tale characters plan a community garden.

Class Project: "Flat Stanley" Letters

Flat Stanley is a wonderful early chapter book for first and second graders. You can easily integrate letter-writing into your social studies or science curriculum by writing letters to family members or other schools to inquire about weather, national parks, cities, famous landmarks, and more.

1. Begin by reading aloud *Flat Stanley* by Jeff Brown (HarperCollins, 1964). Explain that students will each have an opportunity to send off a "Flat Stanley" in the mail to a family member or friend. (Send a note home to children's families explaining the project and requesting the name and address of a family member or friend to whom children can send their Flat Stanley. A sample letter is provided on page 40.)

2. As a class shared writing project, on chart paper create a form letter about the Flat Stanley project. Include information about your class as well as questions for the recipients to answer. Have children copy the letter. Remind them to add the correct salutation and sign their name. (You may also photocopy a class set of the letter, leaving lines for each child to fill in the salutation and closing.)

Student Work

3. Give each child a copy of the "Flat Stanley" Template (page 41). Have students address and stamp an envelope using the information provided by their families, and place their letter and Flat Stanley cutout inside. (Be sure to have contacts available for children whose families do not return the information letter. They might, for example, send their Flat Stanley letters to a classmate or teacher who has moved away.)

Name: _____

Street: _____

City: _____

State: _____ Zip Code: _____

Birthday: _____

Name: _____

Street: _____

City: _____

State: _____ Zip Code: _____

Birthday: _____

Dear Families,

As part of our United States unit of study, we have been reading a fun chapter book series called *Flat Stanley*. This series is about a young boy named Stanley who is accidentally squished "as flat as a pancake" when a bulletin board falls on him. Stanley is very, very flat but otherwise fine. The story goes on to tell how Stanley discovers some real advantages to being flat. He can slide under doors, go into sidewalk grates, and even fold himself up small enough to fit into an envelope and be mailed to California for an exciting vacation.

Next week we plan to mail out plain paper-doll cutouts that we call "Flat Stanleys," to "visit" places in different parts of the United States. We will ask each person who receives a Flat Stanley to "dress" him (using crayons, markers, or other art supplies) in clothes that reflect the local climate and/or activities people do there. We will also ask the person to send back a letter telling what Flat Stanley saw or did in that place, what the climate was like, the distance between that city and ours, and some interesting facts about that location. We will be displaying our Flat Stanleys on a map of the United States. Children will enjoy exploring the display to learn more about the places Flat Stanley visited.

In order to make this project possible, we need your help! Please fill out the information below with the name and address of a friend or family member to whom your child can send his or her Flat Stanley. (Please check with that person first.) Please return this paper by _____.

Sincerely,

~~~~~~

My child may send a Flat Stanley letter to:

Name: _____

Address: _____

_____

_____

On the sign in the image: "Andrew's pumpkin please be careful."

Making Signs

"Mrs. Jensvold, here I come!"

Could that be Andrew's voice I hear down the hallway? It is after school on a fall afternoon and all of the children have left for the day—all but one, Andrew. Andrew comes walking into the classroom pulling a very well-used red wagon carrying a gigantic 70-pound pumpkin. He maneuvers the wagon, backing it into the corner of the room where it will be kept a surprise for the next morning at sharing time. After Andrew leaves, I realize that the stage has been set for a perfect lesson at tomorrow's Writers' Workshop— creating signs. I already know that Andrew and the other children will naturally stumble upon the idea after sharing. All it will take is a few prompts from me to get the ball rolling!

Any time of the year lends itself to making signs. Once you begin the topic of making signs, children will not stop! They will want a sign for the bathroom door that says "Being Used" and they are sure to think of making a sign asking children to "Turn Off the Water When Done" at the fountain. Making signs is a fun, practical way to let children practice writing in real-life situations.

Adapt the sample dialogue that follows, which is based on writing-lesson conversations in my classroom, to introduce and teach this purpose for writing.

Teacher: *Girls and boys, this morning at Morning Meeting, Andrew shared the 70-pound pumpkin that he grew in his garden. I want to remind you that Andrew very nicely asked children to be careful when touching the pumpkin today. He has waited and watched this pumpkin grow all summer long and he does not want anything to happen to his pumpkin while it is staying with us at school. I was wondering if any of you have an idea about how we can use writing to help Andrew.*

Student: *I know! We could label the pumpkin. We could write: "Andrew's Pumpkin, 70 Pounds." That way everyone would know how big the pumpkin really is.*

Student: *Or we could ask people to guess how much the pumpkin weighs. Kind of like a game. And we could say, "Please be careful." Or some signs say, "Please don't touch."*

Teacher: *Those are both very good ideas. What you are both thinking about making is called a sign. People make signs when they want a large group of people to know a piece of information. It is an easier way to tell a large group of people than trying to tell lots of people the information by themselves. I think it would be a great idea to make a sign for Andrew's pumpkin. Turn and talk to a neighbor about some other ideas for what the sign might say.*

[Having children all share with a partner encourages them to be active thinkers and gives everyone a chance to contribute.]

Teacher: *Okay, who has an idea that you or your partner thought of for Andrew's sign?*

Student: *It could say: "Andrew's pumpkin. Please be careful."*

Student: *How about: "Andrew's Pumpkin—70 pounds. No lifting!"*

[In the end, Andrew will decide what to write on the sign—but he will have a lot of helpful input!]

Teacher: *So, today and any day that you are writing, you might want to think about making a sign. Remember, this is a way to let a lot people know information so you don't have to keep telling people the same information over and over again.*

[Send students off to create signs for the classroom or their homes. If they need more direction, brainstorm ideas and post on chart paper.]

Signs are everywhere that children look! Children will love the connections to the real world as they explore and get extra practice with the following ideas.

Writing Size Children often have a difficult time making the letters fit just right on a sign. Their letters are either way too small or way too big. Talk with students about counting the number of words that they plan on putting on their paper. Have them draw a light pencil line for each word on their paper before writing each word. In time, they will become more skilled at fitting words in the space.

Practice Signs Children love to practice writing on dry-erase boards. Give each child a board. Then give children "practice" signs to write. Teach children to think about the words and what size they will be. Signs usually have large letters for ease of reading.

Sign Hunt Go on a short walk around the school and look for signs. Make a chart of reasons people post signs.

Sign	Reason
Exit	To keep people safe
Classroom numbers	To tell people where to go
Lunch choices	So people know which line to stand in

Signs and Symbols Print out several different pictures of signs that include symbols or use a book that shows examples of signs (see Literature Links, page 45). Ask children to look carefully at each sign. Children will notice that signs usually do not have a lot of writing. Many signs use symbols. Make a wall chart of symbols that children might find useful in their writing. Display at the Writing Center.

Book Basket Signs Have students help create signs to label each of the book baskets in the class library. Have them think about the words that will help children know what books are in the baskets as well as the pictures that will help early readers.

Literature Links

Once children become aware of signs and what they say, they can't stop looking for them. The following titles contain lots of examples.

I Read Signs by Tana Hoban (HarperCollins, 1987): Familiar photographed signs fill each page in an easy-to-read manner.

Road Signs: A Harey Race With a Tortoise by Margery Cuyler (Marshall Cavendish, 2008): This fun story is told through road signs rather than traditional text. Along with everyday signs that most children will recognize, there are also funny signs that bring out the humor of the story.

Signs by David Bauer (Coughlan Publishing, 2002): This easy-to-read book is full of photographed signs from every child's surroundings, making it a great resource for children's own sign-making work.

Signs at the Store by Mary Hill (Scholastic, 2003): On a trip to a grocery store, Carly and her dad notice signs that help them find food items as well as how much they cost.

Wanted: Best Friend by A. M. Monson (Scholastic, 1997): When Cat and Mouse have a disagreement about which game they will play, Cat gets upset and leaves. Mouse is certain that he can find a new friend, and sits down to make a sign asking for a "New Best Friend."

Class Project: Signs for School

Take on a larger project by having students create signs for their school. This is a perfect project to complete before your school's Open House.

Student Work

1. Working with partners, have children choose an area of the school and make a sign for it. In addition to making signs for each classroom, children can create signs for a school garden (see sample, right), the lobby (a welcome sign), the cafeteria, the library, and other important places.

2. Children making signs for classrooms can use the Classroom Survey (page 46) to collect important information. They can use the Schoolhouse Template (page 47) as a background for their signs, or create their own symbol.

3. Mount signs on tagboard and laminate, then let children "install" them in the appropriate places.

Name: _____ Date: _____

Classroom Survey

1 What is your teacher's name? _____

2 What is your room number? _____

3 How many kids are in your classroom? _____

4 What are some of your favorite parts of the day?

_____

_____

5 What are some of your class's favorite books?

_____

_____

6 What is something special you are studying?

_____

_____

7 Something else about your class: _____

_____

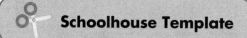

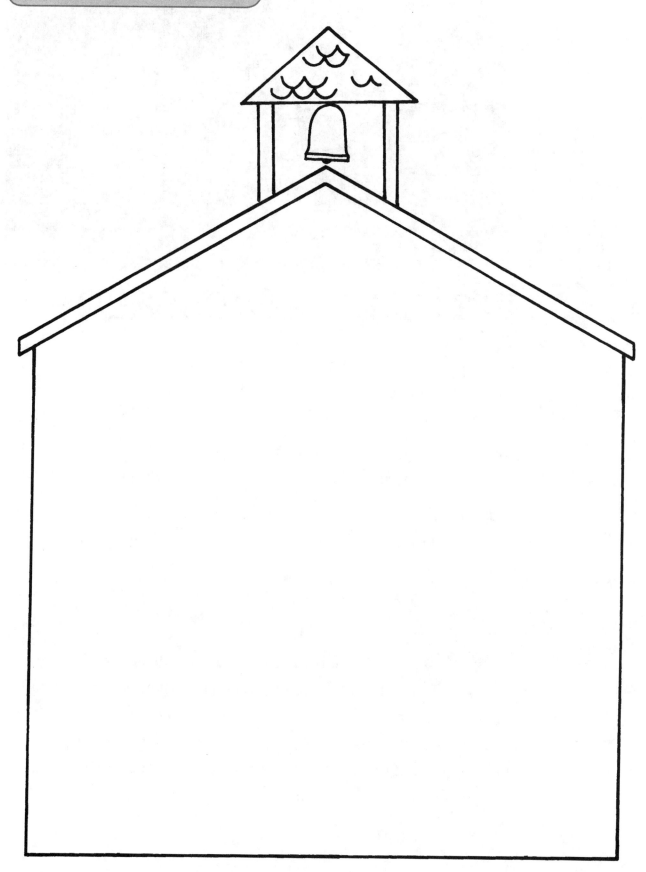

Taking a Message

Ring, ring, ring! "Mrs. Jensvold, the phone is ringing!"
I know, I can hear it, but I am busy helping John
with his zipper that is stuck.

Ring, ring, ring! "Mrs. Jensvold, the phone is ringing!"
I know, but we are right in the middle of our writing lesson.

Ring, ring, ring! "Mrs. Jensvold, the phone is ringing!"
I know, but I can't answer it when Susan is sharing at
Morning Meeting.

We are very fortunate to have telephones in each of our classrooms. Families, teachers, and our wonderful staff in the office can always reach us. However, there are many times when it is inconvenient to stop what we are doing to answer the phone. Having phones in our classrooms inspired a new lesson for real-life writing: taking messages.

Answering telephones and taking accurate messages are skills children need to learn. With more cellular phones and fewer landline phones, children have fewer and fewer opportunities to learn these skills at home. In school with staff members to support children, it is a perfect place to discuss and practice these skills. Taking messages also introduces children to the concept of note-taking, paraphrasing, and determining importance.

Adapt the sample dialogue that follows, which is based on writing-lesson conversations in my classroom, to introduce and teach this purpose for writing.

Teacher: *Do you all remember yesterday when the phone rang and I was busy helping John with his zipper? It was really difficult to stop and get to the phone in time. It probably is like this at your home sometimes, too. If one person is busy, another might answer the phone. I think this idea might work well in our classroom. I was thinking that it might be a good idea for all of us to practice answering the phone and learning how to write a message.*

How many of you answer the phone at home? Wow, it looks like almost all of you! Turn to a partner and share what you say when you answer the phone.

[Allow time for children to take turns pretending to answer the phone.]

Teacher: *Who is ready to share? What do you say when you answer the phone?*

Student: *I say, "Hello, the Smith house."*

Student: *I say, "Hello, this is Sam. Can I help you?"*

Teacher: *Those are both good ideas. How might we answer the phone in our classroom?*

Student: *"Room 16, can I help you?"*

Student: *"Mrs. Jensvold's classroom."*

Teacher: *Those are both good ideas. Now, after you have answered the phone, what happens next?*

Student: *Most of the time the person on the phone needs something. Like, my mom called once to tell me to take the bus home.*

Student: *It might be Mrs. Luck saying that it is indoor recess because it is raining.*

Teacher: *You are exactly right! Usually someone is calling for a specific person to share something important, and it's a good idea to have a way to remember this information. This kind of writing is called taking a message. A telephone message usually includes who the message is for, the name of the person calling, the reason for the call, a return phone number, and a short message. A message also usually includes the name of the person who took the message.*

Student Page

Teacher: *You watch as Mrs. Tavares and I practice. Mrs. Tavares will pretend to call our classroom and I will practice answering the phone and writing a message.*

[I have brought in two old telephones and written out a short script in advance. I also have a message pad handy. (See Message Pad Template, page 52.)]

Do you see how that worked? I started at the top of the message paper and I made sure to get all of the important information. Mrs. Tavares didn't think to give me her phone number but I was sure to ask her for it in case we needed to call her back.

In our classroom, we will spend a few days practicing how to answer the phone and write messages. Then next week, answering the phone will become a job on our Helping Hands chart!

[Copy a supply of the Message Pad Template (page 52) and have children pair up to get started. Place supplies at the Writing Center or dramatic-play center for further practice.]

Follow-Up Mini-Lessons

Student Pages

Children need to become comfortable talking on the phone and listening carefully to the caller in order to record important information. Use the following ideas to stress the importance of listening carefully and paraphrasing information, and to help children gain confidence with this real-life skill.

Telephone Message Mini-Plays Stock a drama station with a couple of old phones and some scripts children can practice reading with a partner. (See Telephone Message Mini-Play, page 53, and May I Take a Message?, page 54. Customize them for your classroom by filling in the blanks as indicated.) Children will love role-playing and their confidence will zoom when it is their real turn to answer the phone.

Writing Names Create a mini-lesson that reminds children that names of people need to be capitalized. Use mini dry-erase boards to have children practice this skill.

Morning Meeting Game Play a game of "Telephone." In advance, create a message form on chart paper. Then start a short message and have each child try to repeat the message to the next person. Continue until the message goes around the circle. Have the last person write the message, then compare it to the original message. Stress the importance of listening carefully!

Paraphrasing Practice A lesson on writing messages can be the beginning of children learning the skill of paraphrasing and note-taking. To practice paraphrasing in another way, have children listen to you as you read aloud information about an animal. Have them tell you the important information that they heard. Stress the importance of putting the information in their own words.

Literature Links

The following titles add a humorous twist to a lesson on writing messages, teaching children the importance of both listening and accuracy!

Listen Buddy by Helen Lester (Harcourt, 1997): Did Buddy listen to his parents when they told him which way to go at the fork in the road? Was it right or left or left or right? What will happen if he goes the wrong way? Buddy learns a lifelong lesson about listening.

Listen Up! Alexander Graham Bell's Talking Machine by Monica Kulling (Random House, 2007): This wonderful nonfiction book tells the history behind the invention of the telephone.

Miss Alaineus: A Vocabulary Disaster by Debra Frasier (Harcourt, 2000): When Sage misses school, she also misses getting the week's 15 vocabulary words. Sage calls her friend and has to quickly write down the words. Does she listen carefully enough to get all 15? What happens when she misses one of the words?

Tell-a-Bunny by Nancy Elizabeth Wallace (Winslow Press, 2000): Every child loves a birthday! When Sunny is planning a party, she calls her friend, who calls another friend, and so on. Soon the message is mixed up and the party is a little bit different than planned.

Class Project: May I Take a Message?

Work together to create a system that works best for your classroom for answering the phone and taking messages. You may decide to rotate this classroom job on a daily or weekly basis.

1. Invite students to use the reproducible Message Pad Template (page 52) as a model for customizing a classroom message pad. Copy a supply and stack next to the phone (you might place the pads in a basket), along with a supply of pens and pencils. You may also want to place a calendar there, to encourage students to record the correct date of any messages they take.

2. Have students work with partners to create scripts for answering the phone. (See May I Take a Message?, page 54.) Let students "perform" their scripts for the class, then decide together what students will say when they answer the phone.

3. Designate a location where children should put the messages they take. This might be a small bulletin board where students can tack up the message, or a message box.

Message Pad

Date: _____

Caller's Name: _____

Calling for: _____

Message: _____

Return Phone Number: _____

Message Pad

Date: _____

Caller's Name: _____

Calling for: _____

Message: _____

Return Phone Number: _____

Telephone Message Mini-Play

Reader 1:   Hello, Room _____. This is [say your name].
            (room #)

            May I help you?

Reader 2:   Yes, this is _____.
                                (name of principal)

            I'm calling for _____.
                                (name of teacher)

Reader 1:   _____ is not available right
                (name of teacher)

            now. May I take a message, please?

Reader 2:   Yes. Please tell _____ that we
                                    (name of teacher)

            have a meeting after school today.

Reader 1:   [Takes message and reads it back.] Is there

            anything else _____?
                                (name of principal)

Reader 2:   No, that's it. Thanks, _____.
                                        (name of Reader 1)

            Have a great day!

Reader 1:   You, too, _____. Bye!
                            (name of principal)

Name: _____   Date: _____

May I Take a Message?

Characters

Reader 1: _____

Reader 2: _____

Reader 1: _____

Reader 2: _____

Reader 1: _____

Reader 2: _____

Reader 1: _____

Reader 2: _____

Reader 1: _____

Reader 2: _____

Lesson
7

Drafting Directions

"Mrs. Jensvold, who will feed our fish while we are away on vacation?"

Usually I leave Mr. Kolbensen a letter and ask that he feed them each day when he is working at school. "How does he know exactly what to feed them?" asked Sarah. That is a good question, a perfect question to answer at writing time! I know that today will be the perfect day for teaching children the skill of writing directions using a how-to format.

Introducing the Lesson

Writing directions or teaching someone how to do something is a skill that is hard for any writer, even adults. Give it a try! Write the directions for making a peanut butter sandwich and ask a colleague to give the directions a try. You are sure to find out that you have forgotten a few important steps or key words. It is the same for children! They need to first choose a topic that they know a lot about, write the steps, have a friend try the steps, and revise. It is a skill that all children can try and all children can improve upon with practice.

Adapt the sample dialogue that follows, which is based on writing-lesson conversations in my classroom, to introduce and teach this purpose for writing.

Teacher: *Girls and boys, Sarah asked a great question this morning at Morning Meeting. When we were getting ready to switch jobs for the week, she noticed that next week we are all on vacation and she is worried about who will feed our fish. Usually when we are away, I ask Mr. Kolbensen to feed the fish. Since we have been learning about writing for many purposes, this is the perfect time to show you about writing directions. We'll write to teach someone how to feed the fish.*

You watch as I think about teaching Mr. Kolbensen how to feed the fish. First I need to pretend to feed the fish so I remember the steps. Okay, now I am ready to write.

[I label a fresh sheet of chart paper "How to Feed the Fish in Room 16."]

Teacher: *Who can tell me what I did first?*

Student: *You found the fish food.*

Teacher: *Right. Since that's the first step, I'm going to write the numeral 1 on my paper. Next to it I will write "First, find the food labeled 'Fish Food.'"*

Then what did I do?

Student: *You took the cap off.*

Teacher: *Okay. I will write that next. That's step number 2, so I start on a new line, and write "2." Now I am ready to write the next direction: "Next, twist off the cap."*

What should I put for step 3?

Student: *You need to tell him how much food to pinch.*

Teacher: *How about this? "3. Use two fingers to pinch a small amount of food."*

What should I write last?

Student: *You need to tell him to squish the food. If you leave big flakes, the fish won't eat the food.*

Teacher: *Does this sound right? "4. Squish the food between your fingers and sprinkle over the top of the water." There, I'm finished!*

Student: *I think you better add to open and close the lid of the tank. We don't want the fish to jump out!*

Teacher: *Good idea. Talk with your writing partner about where I could add that information.*

[Listen as children discuss how to add new information, particularly someplace other than at the end of the directions.]

Teacher: *I hear lots of good thoughts. I will go back to step 1 and add: "Open the top of the tank." And then I will add a new step at the end, step 5, and write: "Close the lid." I'm also going to draw a quick sketch next to each step to show him what to do. Now let's read all the directions, one step at a time, and make sure we have included everything someone needs to know about feeding the fish.*

[You might invite a volunteer to act out the steps for a more concrete review of the directions.]

Teacher: *You are all experts at many things. Some of you know how to draw snakes, some of you know how to feed dogs, some of you know how to make paper airplanes. Some of you even know how to make chocolate chip cookies! Right now, turn to your partner and share three things that you are good at. Think about which one you could write how-to directions for.*

[Allow time for students to share their ideas.]

I heard lots of interesting things. Today for writing, you will all take at least one of your ideas, use our new writing paper, and write a "How To" piece.

[Copy a supply of the reproducible "How-To" Directions Template (page 60) and walk children through how to use it before they get started.]

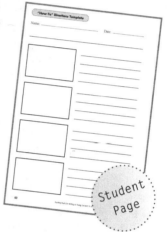

Student Page

Follow-Up Mini-Lessons

Children need lots of practice with writing how-to pieces. They need specific examples of how to make their work more detailed. They need to learn how to work with a partner to try out their how-to pieces to make sure their directions make sense and are clear. The ideas listed here will help children get extra practice with all these skills.

Transition Words Teach another mini-lesson on using transition words such as *first, next, then, last*. Have children revise an old piece of writing by adding the key transition words to the text.

Caution! Some how-to pieces could use warnings such as "Make sure there is an adult to help." Encourage children to write these "warnings" on sticky notes and place them in the correct spot. Lots of books by Gail Gibbons include warnings.

Try It Out Teach children that when they are done writing a how-to piece, to try it out on a friend. As they read, their partner should try each step. This can be tricky. Be sure to model this in front of the whole group. Children can read their how-to directions and you can act out each step. Discuss how to make changes where they are needed.

Add Number Words Teach a mini-lesson on adding number words to a piece of writing—for example, "Draw a 1-inch line" or "Make two eyes." Using number words is a great way to make directions more specific and to reinforce math concepts in the process.

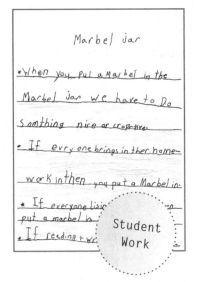

Marbel jar

*When you pul a Marbel in the Marbel jar we have to Do samthing nice or creptive.

* If evry one brings in ther home- work in then you put a Marbel in.

* If everyone lisin ... put a marbel in.

* If reading + wr...

Student Work

Origami Art Using a direction-based book on origami (see Literature Links, below), have children fold paper to create a simple form, such as a basic airplane or hat. Discuss what was most helpful in the directions (words and diagrams). Make a wall chart listing key "direction" words and identifying helpful features in pictures.

Literature Links

Many nonfiction books have how-to sections intertwined within the text. These sections often follow at the end of the regular text as an "extra." Often, one how-to section can serve as a tool for many mini-lessons.

Apples by Gail Gibbons (Holiday House, 2001): This book explains how apples grow, lists different types of apples, and ends with a page on how to make an apple pie. This book is full of possibilities for multiple writing lessons.

How to Lose All Your Friends by Nancy Carlson (Penguin, 1994): Children will love this "backward" approach as they laugh their way through undesirable behaviors and six easy steps to losing your best friends.

The Pumpkin Book by Gail Gibbons (Holiday House, 2000): Beautiful illustrations and easy-to-read words make this nonfiction book perfect for teaching many text features, including how-to directions. The book ends with a page dedicated to "How to Carve a Pumpkin."

The Usborne Book of Origami by Eileen O'Brien (EDC Publishing, 1997): Step-by-step instructions accompanied by illustrations help children learn how to turn a plain sheet of paper into a beautiful piece of artwork.

Class Project: How to Draw

Children love to draw. Almost every child feels proud of being able to draw something—an animal, a special flower, a funny face, or a flag. With a class How-To book, children can explain to others how they do it!

1. Have children think about something that they are good at drawing. Encourage them to go through the steps to remember what they do to make that drawing.

2. Using the "How-To" Directions Template (page 60), have children create a set of directions telling how to make their drawings. Remind them to number their steps.

3. Publish their work in a large class book titled *How to Draw* by Room _____. Invite the librarian to display the book in the library with other drawing books.

Teaching Tip

This is also a great project to tie into a science or social studies curriculum. If your class is studying birds, have them create a book about how to draw different birds. If your class is studying the United States, have students create a book about how to draw flags from different states.

Student Work

"How-To" Directions Template

Name: _____ Date: _____

_____

Teaching Real-Life Writing to Young Learners © 2010 by Paula Jensvold. Scholastic Teaching Resources

Lesson 8

Journaling

In preparation for a lesson on journaling, I greet my students in the morning with this question: "What's the news?" I give everyone a quiet minute to think about something they might share in response to this question at our Morning Meeting. And I remind them that it can be a very small bit of news like a soccer game coming up or having your dog chew your sock, or something larger like a special birthday celebration.

This greeting is a favorite of my second graders and we use it almost every week. That is why after only a few months, we transition into using journals titled "What's the News?" These journals act as way to record the same bits of information in a quick and easy way that will later act as ideas for "small-moment" stories. (See page 83 for a writing lesson on small moments.)

Journal-writing can be a challenge for children of all ages. Children often feel that they don't have "anything" to write. They often have a difficult time writing down feelings or reasons for feeling the way they do. They often finish early and say, "I'm all done." Journal-writing is a skill that we need to "teach" children on a regular basis in a manageable way. We need to give them strategies for learning what to write and how to write it.

Adapt the sample dialogue that follows, which is based on writing-lesson conversations in my classroom, to introduce and teach this purpose for writing.

Teaching Tip

Student Page

To make "What's the News?" journals for students., copy the reproducible Journal Paper Template (page 65). Stack a dozen or so pages together for each journal and add a construction-paper cover, then staple to bind. Have children write the title "What's the News?" on the cover, sign their name, and decorate as they wish.

Teacher: *I noticed that many of you have been having a difficult time thinking of ideas to write about during Writers' Workshop. I was thinking that I know all of you have stories to tell because when we use our "What's the News?" greeting in the morning, you all have important things to share! This weekend I made a "What's the News?" journal for each of you. Today I will show you how to use your journal to record things that happen every day!*

Each time we write in your journal, it will be important to write the date in the upper right corner. This is important because it helps remind us of when the special event happened or when you chose to write about it.

[Take a moment to show the upper right corner of a journal.]

Teacher: *Next, I would like you all to think of a piece of news that you shared this morning at Morning Meeting. I will give you three minutes to write. Write the words just like you would if you were sharing the news by speaking it instead. Ready, set, write!*

[Allow several minutes for children to write in their journals. Remind students as needed about the news they shared at Morning Meeting.]

Teacher: *Wow! Many of you are having a hard time stopping! See how easy it is to write your news? And remember, news can be anything special, funny, happy, sad, important, unusual, or embarrassing that is happening to you.*

Today when you go off to write a new small-moment story, remember, you can always go to your "What's the News?" journal and use an entry as the beginning of a story or a way to get an idea.

[Rather than having students write in their "What's the News?" journals during Writers' Workshop, encourage them to use their journals throughout the day to record ideas, and then as a resource during writing time.]

During the lesson on journaling, children learn to write as part of their day. Be sure to have your students do exactly that: write every day. Keep children's journals close by so that at any moment they can grab them and record a moment. Model this type of writing yourself in a class journal. Use the following ideas to help your journal mini-lessons stay fresh and full of good content.

Write Every Day!
Use your journals throughout the day, not just at writing time. After an interesting science experiment, have children get their journals out and write about what happened. When children lose teeth, have them quickly jot down the stories in their journals. Using journals throughout the day will help children see that writing fits into their everyday lives. It will also show them that they have lots of ideas for small-moment stories.

Don't Forget the Date
Teach a quick mini-lesson on how to write the date or where to start on the page. Model for children different styles or formats for writing the date, including numerically by month/day/year (11/23/10 or 11/23/2010) and spelling out the month (November 23, 2010).

Highlight
After several entries, encourage children to use a yellow highlighter to call out important words in their journals, such as the names of people or places.

Creating Lists
Use mini-lessons to explore list-writing, a helpful source of ideas for journaling. Possible list-starters include:

* Name five important people
* Name five things that make you feel happy
* List five places that you have visited
* Name five signs of spring [summer, fall, winter]

Class Journal
If having your children write in their own journals regularly is a difficult task to fit in, keep a class journal. When something funny, surprising, or eventful happens in your class, take out your class journal and create an entry together. When children are stuck for ideas during writing time, encourage them to use the class journal to discover an idea.

Teaching Tip

For two more examples of journals to use, see Science Journals (page 89) and Conversation Journals (page 90).

Literature Links

Children learn best about journaling through reading journaling stories. By listening to journal entries, they begin to hear how the entries start, how often the entries are written, and what important information is included in an entry. Try these books to provide students with the experience of listening to published journaling.

Birdie's Lighthouse by Deborah Hopkinson (Atheneum, 1997): When Birdie moves to an island off the coast of Maine, her only friend is her diary. In her diary she writes about her family and the important things that she learns from her father, a lighthouse keeper.

Diary of a Worm by Doreen Cronin (HarperCollins, 2003): Did you ever wonder what it is like to be a worm? This hilarious book tells children just what it is like. Worms go to school, play with friends, and live with their parents. This book is a perfect way to help children understand the simple things that can go in a journal.

Notebook Know-How: Strategies for the Writer's Notebook by Aimee Buckner (Stenhouse, 2005): This is a wonderful teacher-resource book full of ideas for journaling with children.

Class Project: Memory Book

Create a class memory book that follows a "journal" format.

1. Using large "big-book" paper, journal about special events that happen throughout the school year—for example, a field trip, a class performance, a special visitor, or children's birthdays. Assign each entry to a small group of children (or a pair of children). Include photographs and have children create captions.

2. Keep the big book in your class library for children to read as it is created and also to get ideas for their own writing. Teach children how to take an entry from the class journal and turn it into a story by following these steps:

   ❊ Read an entry

   ❊ Think about the event

   ❊ Decide how you fit into the story

   ❊ Tell your own story

Student Work

   Children will need lots of practice with this skill of taking an idea from an entry and turning it into an idea for a story. Using a class journal is a perfect way to model this skill in either a large- or small-group setting.

Date: _____

_____

_____

_____

_____

_____

_____

_____

_____

_____

_____

Lesson 9

Designing Ads

"Mrs. Jensvold, can I go to the Schoolmate Store?" asked Brian. "I noticed that they are having a sale: buy two pens and get the third free. I have just enough money!"

"Sounds like a deal." I ask if anyone noticed something else that's happening at the school store this week.

"I did!" said Sarah. "They are having a raffle. You can win a stuffed bunny. All you have to do is spend $1 to go toward charity and your name gets put in the raffle."

I asked Sarah how she heard about the raffle.

"I saw an ad on the front door!"

After our exchange that morning, a writing lesson on designing ads seemed only natural. This lesson combines a playfulness with language and elements of art and inventive thinking, making it a favorite with students. Because each word is an important part of an advertisement, this lesson also invites exploration of specific language.

Introducing the Lesson

Ads are everywhere we look! They're in stores, in windows, in the paper, on buses and subways, on billboards, and on TV. Children are quick to recognize words in advertisements. *New, now, free, easy, amazing, introducing, special offer, bargain,* and *hurry* are just a few of the most common words used in advertising. If children are surrounded by ads, it only makes sense to let them put their knowledge to use in their own writing—in ads they create!

Adapt the sample dialogue that follows, which is based on writing-lesson conversations in my classroom, to introduce and teach this purpose for writing.

Teacher: *Today when Brian came into the classroom, he asked to go to the Schoolmate Store. Brian, tell your classmates about your purchase.*

Student: *I bought two pens and they gave me a third one for free!*

Teacher: *How did you know that you would get a free pen?*

Student: *I saw a sign on the front door when I came into school. It said, "Buy two pens and get the third one free." And I had enough money!*

Teacher: *The sign that Brian saw was a special kind of sign called an advertisement. The sign was designed to encourage children to shop at the school store this week. Next week, there might be another advertisement. Maybe pencil sharpeners will be on sale.*

People make advertisements to get the attention of other people. Let me show you what I mean by sharing this book. This book is called Pet Show! *Can you guess what this book might be about by looking at the cover?*

Student: *I bet there is a pet show in town and that little boy wants to go.*

Student: *It looks like he is wondering whether or not he can win. See, the sign says* prizes.

Teacher: *You are both right. The cover of this book pictures an advertisement for an upcoming pet show. Let's read to see what happens.*

[I read the book slowly, letting the children enjoy the story. Then I turn back to the cover.]

Teacher: *So, what do you notice about the advertisement? What information does it give us?*

Student: *It gives the day of the week, Saturday.*

Student: *And the time, 11 o'clock.*

Teacher: *What part of the advertisement is easiest to read?*

Student: *The part that says* Pet Show! *The letters are really big and bright orange.*

Teacher: *That's right. Usually the most important part of the advertisement is written in the largest letters.*

Today we are going to design advertisements. I want you all to think of a favorite place. When you have your idea, raise your hand to let us know you are ready.

[Children will need a few minutes to think of an idea. If I don't see a lot of hands, I encourage children to turn and talk with a neighbor about their places.]

Teacher: *Okay, who is ready to share?*

Student: *I love to get ice cream at Al's.*

Student: *I went to the bookstore and got the new Harry Potter book this week.*

Student: *My dad and I went to the park to try out the new climbing bars.*

Teacher: *Great! It sounds like you all have ideas. Today we are going to work on making an advertisement for those places you're thinking about.*

[I model my own ad design on a large sheet of paper, thinking aloud about word choice, the size of my letters, and a picture.]

Teacher: *To start, I put the name of one of my favorite places at the top, just like on the cover of* Pet Show! *Underneath the name, I'm going to list a few different things that I like about this spot, or what they sell. Let's see, I think I will write* ice cream, grilled cheese sandwiches, french fries, *and* hamburgers. *I'm also going to write the best time to go. I will write "Come on Saturday for lunch." There, now I am ready for color and a few small pictures!*

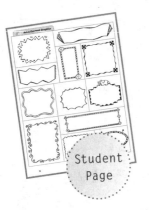

Student Page

[Introduce the reproducible Advertisement Graphics (page 70) and model how to incorporate one of the graphics into your sample ad. Give children copies of these reproducible graphics as they prepare to create their own ads. They will have fun incorporating these real-life ad graphics into their designs. (You may wish to enlarge this page before using to provide more space for writing.)]

Follow-Up Mini-Lessons

Children love to make advertisements! Spend the extra time to help them with simple tasks such as writing with creative lettering, making straight lines, and using a thesaurus. These skills will make a world of difference in their published pieces.

Local Brochures Collect brochures from local businesses and pass them out to students. Ask students what they notice about the lettering, colors, and pictures. What stands out the most? Does every advertisement have a picture?

Different Letters: Teach children how to make different-style letters. Bubble letters are always a favorite for youngsters but take a lot of practice. A mini-lesson on making bubble letters will be a big hit. (For one method, see page 28.) Have them go further, writing their names with three different types of lettering.

Teaching Real-Life Writing to Young Learners

Stencils Introduce stencils, demonstrating how to use them, and add different-size and different-shape letter stencils to your Writing Center.

Straight Lines Teach children how to use a ruler. Hold the ruler with one hand and draw along the edge with the other hand. Provide scrap paper and let children practice making horizontal, vertical, and diagonal lines.

Thesaurus When teaching word choice for advertisements, introduce children to using a thesaurus. Brainstorm key words that they are using a lot and look up those words in a thesaurus to find new interesting words. Keep a list of these new words on a bulletin board or wall chart to encourage variety in word choice and correct spelling.

Literature Links

Children learn best about advertisements by looking at good examples. If examples in literature are difficult to find, collect advertisements from your local bookstores, newspapers, and post offices (for example, ads announcing new stamps). Display these examples along with the following book titles.

Minnie and Moo: Wanted Dead or Alive by Denys Cazet (HarperCollins, 2006): Minnie and Moo are mistaken for bank robbers. The cover shows a detailed advertisement for a reward that will be given to anyone with information. Children will love this mixed-up story!

Pet Show! by Ezra Jack Keats (Puffin Books, 1972): The pet show is starting and Archie cannot find his cat! The colorful cover offers a great example of an ad, and includes important information, such as the date and time of the pet show.

Class Project: Ads for School

Children like nothing better than seeing their work displayed on the walls of the school. Arrange for your class to take over the responsibility of creating advertisements for an event or other purpose. Possibilities include:

School Store: Work with the group to create posters advertising different products that are available. Have children include names of items, prices, and times that the school store is open. They'll want to create special ads to announce special savings and sales.

Lost and Found: Have children take an item from the school's Lost and Found and make a "Found" ad. Have them include a description of the item, the size, and where it is being stored until it is claimed.

Invitations

*"Mrs. Jensvold, I wasn't invited to Sam's party and now my feelings
are hurt."*

*"I don't think kids should be allowed to invite other kids to parties
unless everyone is invited!"*

How many times in a school year do you have this
conversation with children in your classroom? A good way
to respond is by sharing *I'm Not Invited?* by Diana Cain Bluthenthal
(Atheneum, 2003). Then try the lesson that follows to give every
child an opportunity to be involved in making invitations and
celebrating at school.

Teaching
Tip

If students will be mailing invitations they create in class, gather addresses in advance of this lesson. See Teaching Tip, page 34, for information on creating address books.

Teaching about invitations can be a difficult thing in school. Invitations are typically "at home" writing experiences because they deal mainly with celebrations such as birthdays. Many children have received an invitation at some time in the mail. And writing their own invitations is always an exciting experience, because it usually signals a special event is about to happen.

Adapt the sample dialogue that follows, which is based on writing-lesson conversations in my classroom, to introduce and teach this purpose for writing.

Teacher: *Yesterday I got something special in the mail that I wanted to share with you all today. It is an invitation to a bar mitzvah. A bar mitzvah is a religious celebration. Look at the invitation. It tells who the celebration is for, where the celebration will be, on what day it will be, and what time. All of the important information is listed here. There is also another card with the invitation. It is called a response card. Sometimes people include a response card, other times people ask you to RSVP, which means to call to tell if you are coming to the party or not.*

Have any of you ever received an invitation in the mail?

Student: *I have, to a birthday party.*

Student: *Me too! My cousin sent out a* Star Wars *card.*

Teacher: *Today we will learn how to make special invitations. Do you all remember that we are just ending our unit of study on peacemakers in history? I was thinking that it might be a good idea to have a celebration of our learning. I thought that your families might enjoy seeing and hearing about what you have learned in this unit. Today we will make an invitation to invite someone special to come to school to see what we've learned.*

Student: *When will it be?*

Teacher: *That is a great question! Let's keep track here on the easel of the important things we need to include in the invitation.*

[Begin to list on chart paper important information, beginning with the nature of the celebration and the date.]

Teacher: *What else do you think we need to put in the invitation? Turn and tell a friend your ideas.*

[Give children plenty of time to generate information that they will need to include in their invitations.]

Teacher: *I heard lots of great ideas! Who would like to share?*

Student: *The time, we have to tell our families what time to come so we aren't at lunch.*

Student: *We should put our room number.*

Teacher: *Great. I will add these ideas to our list. Maybe we should also tell them why they are coming.*

Student: *Oh yeah! Like "A Peacemaker Celebration."*

Student: *We should also have them tell us if they can come or not. My mom works, she probably won't be able to come.*

Teacher: *Good idea! Along with the information, I think we should add some kind of picture. What kinds of pictures or illustrations would go with an invitation for a peacemakers celebration?*

Student: *Maybe a picture of a peacemaker who we have studied.*

Student: *Maybe a dove, a symbol of peace.*

Teacher: *Those are both great ideas. The decision of a picture will be yours today. Here is the paper that you will be making your invitation on. Notice the words what, when, where. Your job today will be to fill in the information and then decorate the paper. When you are finished with your invitations, we will put them in envelopes, then address the envelopes, place stamps on them, and put them in the mailbox.*

[Give each child a copy of an Invitation Template (pages 75–76).]

Student Pages

Follow-Up Mini-Lessons

It can be tricky to teach children the craft of making invitations at school. Instead of focusing so much on making invitations, teach the skills that they will need to use when they are making invitations at home. The following mini-lessons help build word skills.

High-Frequency Word Practice Children need to learn how to spell the key words that make up an invitation, such as *who, what, where, when, why,* and *time.* Write each word on an index card. Let children sort the words by characteristics (such as "starts with *wh*" and "doesn't start with *wh*"). Add the words to the weekly spelling list and the class Word Wall. Play games such as Guess My Word, and encourage children to pay attention to the shape of each word. If children learn how to spell these words correctly, it will make creating invitations much easier!

Reading Response Read lots of fiction stories about invitations. (See Literature Links, page 74.) As a follow-up to a read-aloud, have children make a pretend invitation that goes along with the book. This will reinforce the use of language in invitations.

Share Invitations Write a letter to families inviting them to send in examples of invitations. Have children look closely at each one and share what they notice. Are they all birthday invitations or do people send out invitations for other reasons? What words tell what the invitation is for?

Literature Links

Use these fun titles to give children a better understanding of invitations and their purposes.

A Letter to Amy by Ezra Jack Keats (HarperCollins, 1968): Peter wants to invite Amy to his birthday party, but he wants it to be a surprise.

Angelina's Invitation to the Ballet by Katharine Holabird (Penguin, 2007): Angelina is the winner of two tickets to a ballet. Who will she take? Pull out different pieces of writing from six envelopes to find out!

I'm Not Invited? by Diana Cain Bluthenthal (Atheneum, 2003): When Minni is not invited to Charles's party, her feelings are hurt. Through lists, letters, and conversation, she is reminded of birthdays for the whole week. Children learn that a simple misunderstanding can cause a lot of problems!

Miss Spider's Tea Party by David Kirk (Scholastic, 1994): Miss Spider tries her best to host a tea party but everyone is afraid to come because they might be eaten. Then, thanks to one small moth, Miss Spider gets to host a delightful party for 12.

Class Project: A Celebration of Learning

In addition to celebrating learning at the end of a unit of study, there are many other occasions throughout the school year when an invitation is appropriate. Children can send invitations to families for Open School Night, conferences, a class play, an evening of art and music, and other special events. A lesson on writing invitations provides the perfect opportunity for creating sets of invitations to keep on hand for events that occur throughout the school year.

1. Consult a school calendar with children and make a list of school events.

2. Assign small groups one event. Provide children with basic information for the event, and have them work together to create an invitation.

3. Make a class set of each invitation. File the invitations so they are ready to send out when the event approaches.

You're Invited!

What: _____

When: _____

_____

Where: _____

_____

_____

RSVP: _____

Invitation Template

Directions: To make a double-sided card, cut out the template, fold on the center line, and glue the backs together.

What: ________

When: ________

____

Where: ________

____

____

RSVP: ________

Fold Here

You're Invited!

Making a Map

"I can't wait for tomorrow! We finally get to go on our field trip!"

The chatter is lively at the end of the day. Tomorrow we will go on a field trip, by foot, to the community library. For many children, it is the first time they have been to this library.

As a way to encourage children to sign out books from our public library, each year I take my students to the community library to get library cards. The librarian gives the children a tour, reads a book, and explains how to check out a book. After we go on our trip, I make sure to plan for a few mini-lessons on mapping. After all, on our way to the library, we will notice the details that a town map is made of—roads, landmarks, shopping centers, schools, parks, and more.

Introducing the Lesson

Children love to make maps, but it can often be a frustrating and overwhelming task. Try starting a lesson by sharing *My Map Book* to help children understand that they can all make a map.

Adapt the sample dialogue that follows, which is based on writing-lesson conversations in my classroom, to introduce and teach this purpose for writing.

Teacher: *Do you all remember our field trip to the library last week? As I was walking to the library, I was thinking of all the stores and places that I noticed along the way. We passed restaurants, stores, another school, the fire department, and lots of houses. Taking that walk got me thinking a lot about maps and another reason why people write. Oftentimes people will write directions or make a map to show where a place is located. Today I will teach you how to use your writing to create a map.*

Let's take a look at this book. It is called My Map Book. *You probably noticed right away from the cover that these are maps that have been made by other children. I think you will be surprised when we open the book to find all the different things that you can show with a map.*

[As I read through each page, I pause and ask children about what they see. There is a map of a dog, a bedroom, and a heart, among other things not usually mapped. By the end of the book, most children are very excited about having an opportunity to create a map of their own.]

Teacher: *Now that we have finished the book, who has an idea of a map that they could make? Turn and talk with a neighbor about an idea or two.*

[Give children plenty of time to share ideas with their partners.]

Student: *I know: I want to make a map of my dinner table. We all have our own spots and my mom makes really great food!*

Student: *I think I want to make a map of my heart. I have a sad spot where my dog died but a really happy spot where I play soccer.*

Teacher: *Today we will make maps. I will give each of you a large sheet of paper. Start by using a pencil. Don't forget to add labels to your maps. We will stop when our pencil sketches are done and tomorrow we will learn how to add color and a title.*

Follow-Up Mini-Lessons

The following extensions will help children add detail and meaning to their maps. Simple things such as adding a title and using symbols can make creating a map manageable and more accurate.

Give It a Title Teach a mini-lesson on making a title for a map. Have children use a separate sheet of paper, a sentence strip, or an index card so that it does not interfere with their drawing. Teach them to use different colors so that their title stands out from the rest of their map.

Create a Key Some maps have keys. Teach children the purpose of a key. Explain that sometimes if there is a lot of one thing, such as trees, a writer will use a symbol that represents the item instead of drawing each and every one. This is a good time to introduce the Map Symbols (page 81) and review which symbols stand for a single item on a map (such as the hospital symbol) and which could represent more than one of something. For example, the symbol of several trees could stand for a wooded area.

Map the Classroom If Open House is around the corner, encourage children to create a map of the classroom that they will use to show their families around. Have them label important places and objects that they want their parents to be sure to see.

Playground Map Take the children outside and have them create a map of the playground. Using graph paper can help children begin to explore scale.

Literature Links

Children will need lots of experiences with maps. They need to examine features on maps, learn to recognize symbols, and create their own maps. The following titles give children the experience and models that they need to be successful.

A Bird's Eye View by Marcia S. Freeman (Rand McNally, 1999): Dramatic illustrations give a unique perspective of a neighborhood, a baseball diamond, and many other places around the world.

Me on the Map by Joan Sweeney (Random House, 1998): A young girl introduces readers to cartography, beginning with crayon drawings of her home and expanding into the world beyond.

My Map Book by Sara Fanelli (HarperCollins, 1995): With its collection of nontraditional maps, including bedrooms, hearts, and dogs, this book gives the word *map* a new meaning that is just right for kids!

National Geographic Big Book of Maps (National Geographic Society, 2001): These beautifully detailed maps are perfect to share with the whole class. The book begins with a neighborhood map and continues on to maps of each continent and a world map.

There's a Map on My Lap! All About Maps by Tish Rabe (Random House, 2002): Young readers get a lesson on maps from the Cat in the Hat, who introduces different kinds of maps, map formats, and map symbols.

Class Project: Map the Neighborhood

Make a map of your town! Children will enjoy sharing their knowledge of the neighborhood and will revisit this special map again and again to tour their town.

1. First share with children an example of a neighborhood or town map. *National Geographic Big Book of Maps* (see Literature Links, page 79) is a perfect introduction for this lesson.

2. Explain to children that they will be working together to create a map of their town. Together, brainstorm and list places in your town, such as the fire station, library, school, hospital, banks, playgrounds, parks, and grocery stores.

3. Place a clear shower curtain on the floor and explain that it will be the background for the map. Work with students to plot out the streets. Label each street with a permanent marker.

4. Give children precut white paper and have them select a building or item from the list to draw. Use contact paper or clear tape to fasten the drawings to the back of the shower curtain.

5. Have children add details such as trees, cars, road signs, and a compass rose for showing and reading directions on a map.

Teaching Tip

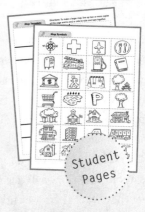

Student Pages

Children will benefit from applying what they learned in the class project to create individual maps of their town or neighborhood. Stock the Writing Center with copies of the Map Symbols (page 81) and Map Template (page 82). Review the Map Symbols with children, then demonstrate how to cut out and tape together multiple copies of the Map Template to create a larger map. (Show students how to line up copies of the template end-to-end or side-to-side before they tape them together.)

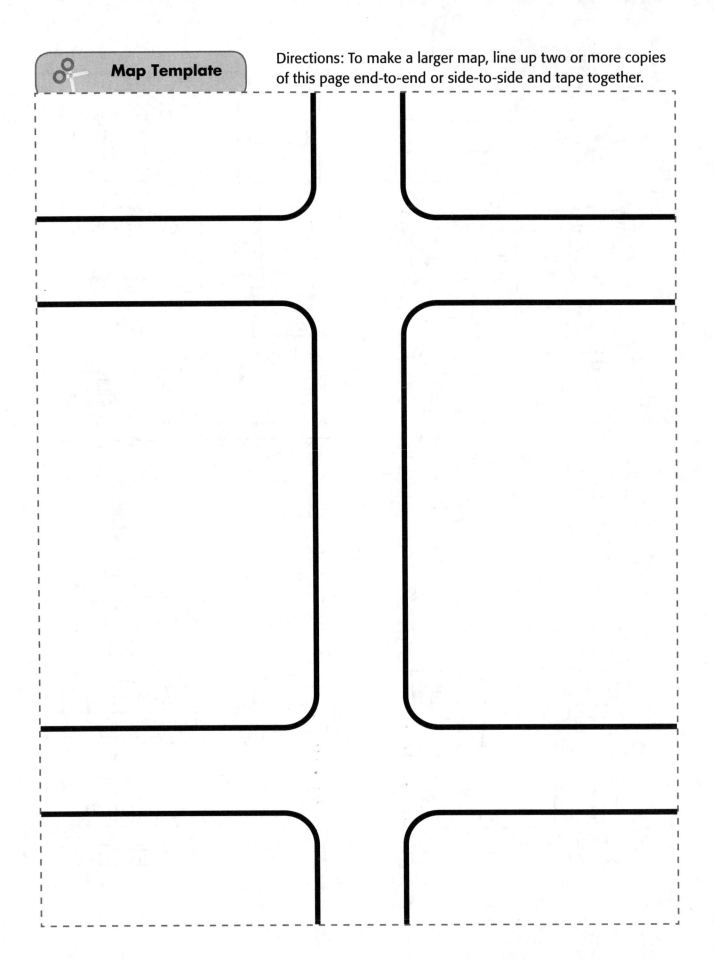

Map Template

Directions: To make a larger map, line up two or more copies of this page end-to-end or side-to-side and tape together.

Teaching Real-Life Writing to Young Learners © 2010 by Paula Jensvold. Scholastic Teaching Resources

Crafting a Small Moment

"Oh my goodness! It's a snake! Quick everybody, look at the snake!"

All of the children are outside in the schoolyard playing a game and learning about spiders after a science lesson. Nobody is looking for a snake. Especially me! When everyone sees the snake trying to get through our classroom door, and we all run in the opposite direction. I know that this will be a perfect class story to write during our next Writers' Workshop. Writing stories to share small moments such as this (and quieter moments, too) is a wonderful real-life reason for writing.

Introducing the Lesson

Elementary classrooms are full of small-moment stories! Any time a tooth pops out, a special guest arrives, or one of us brings something amazing in for sharing, a story is ready to be written. As a teacher, pay particular attention to these small moments so that you can encourage children to write them down. Children often think they need a "big" something to write about. Nothing is further from the truth! We want children to zoom in like a camera and write about all the small things that happen in their lives.

Adapt the sample dialogue that follows, which is based on writing-lesson conversations in my classroom, to introduce and teach this purpose for writing.

Teacher: *Yesterday we had a very exciting science lesson. We were all very busy learning about spiders. We learned that spiders do not have very good eyesight, then we all went outside to play a game to learn more about this. During the game, some of you were spiders with your eyes closed and others were insects coming into the webs. The game was going well, then all of a sudden . . .*

Student: *Amy saw a snake and yelled!*

Teacher: *That is exactly what happened! Do you remember how some of you ran away from the snake and some of you went closer to have a look?*

Student: *I remember that it was really close to our classroom door and I was worried it was going to go inside.*

Teacher: *Me too! I was one of those people who went in the opposite direction.*

After school yesterday, I was talking with some teachers and telling them our story. Then I realized this makes a great small-moment story! Today I will teach you how to write down a small moment.

First I will need our story-writing paper. It has three pages stapled together. It will help me remember that I need a beginning, a middle, and an end to my story. Next, I will draw my pictures. Turn to a neighbor and share what you think my first picture should be.

I heard lots of great things. I agree with most of you. I will make my first picture of us all playing our spider game. Let's see, what happened next?

Student: *Amy saw the snake and yelled, "Snake!"*

Teacher: *Good thinking. I think in my picture I will draw Amy with a speech bubble. I will also draw the snake. The background of my picture will be our outside classroom door. I want to be sure to mention that it was really close to getting inside the school!*

Now I am on page 3. How should I end my story? Turn and tell a friend.

[Give children plenty of time to share ideas with their partners.]

Student: *I think you should put a picture of us walking around the school to a different door. Remember, we didn't come back through our classroom door. The snake was too close.*

Teacher: *You're right. We walked around the school in a line and came in the side door. Everyone was yelling and was really excited about the snake. Cole even said that it was the first real snake he had ever seen! Now I am ready for my words. You watch as I write.*

[Since the children have had time to talk and are familiar with what happened, go through this part quickly. The idea of the lesson is to get them writing their own small-moment stories.]

Teacher: *Did you all see what I did today as a writer? I first thought of something that recently happened. It was something exciting that happened to our class that I knew other people would enjoy reading about. Right now, think about your day at school. Have you recently won a game in math? Forgot your lunch and had to eat something that you didn't like very much? Finished your first chapter book? Or lost a tooth? All of these ideas would make great small-moment stories. Turn and tell someone a story that you are thinking about writing today.*

[Let children share ideas with a partner, then with the class. Give children copies of the Small-Moments Writing Paper (page 87) and let them create their own small-moment stories.]

Student Page

Follow-Up Mini-Lessons

Writing a good small-moment story takes lots of practice with lots of specific instruction. Make sure to teach several mini-lessons on small skills that will produce big results. Use these follow-up lessons as ways to target skills that are doable for children.

Zoom! Teach children to zoom in like a camera. Children often want to write about the whole day. Encourage them to select one small thing that happened and write about that event with more detail. Use the book *Zoom* by Istvan Banyai (Viking, 1995) to show how to zoom in on a topic.

The Three Ps If children are having a difficult time generating ideas, teach them the three Ps: they can always write about a special person, pet, or place. Revisit picture books for examples of how authors use "the three Ps." Children will find many examples. Have children make lists of special people, pets, and places to use as a writing reference.

An Author's Ideas Marc Brown is a perfect author to study if you are teaching children where to get ideas. In many interviews, he tells his audience that he gets most of his ideas from his children and things that happen to them in real life, such as loosing a tooth, going to camp, and taking family vacations.

Good Beginning/Good Ending Encourage children to look at books and study how authors begin and end their stories. Pass out several books and have children just read the first pages. Generate a list of words authors often use to begin a story (*one day, in the morning, my favorite*). Try the same thing to explore endings.

Literature Links

It can sometimes be difficult to find good "small-moment" stories that are written in a personal narrative format. Look for books that show examples of small events that your children can relate to such as saying goodbye to a loved one, copying a big sister, having a sleepover, or preparing for the first day of school.

Do Like Kyla by Angela Johnson (Orchard Books, 1990): A little sister spends the day imitating her big sister. That is, until Kyla imitates her little sister in the end.

The Good-Bye Book by Judith Viorst (Simon & Schuster, 1992): A little boy does everything he can think of to convince his parents to stay home instead of go out to a restaurant. But before he knows it, his parents have left and he is happily reading with his babysitter.

Owl Moon by Jane Yolen (Penguin, 1987): One snowy evening, a girl and her father travel into the snowy woods to find a great horned owl.

Shortcut by Donald Crews (HarperCollins, 1996): A group of children knows that they are not supposed to take the "shortcut" home on the train tracks. One night when they are running late, they take the shortcut. All seems to fine until they hear a train coming.

The Snowy Day by Ezra Jack Keats (Puffin, 1962): Every child loves the first snowfall of the year. Peter can't wait to get in his snowsuit and explore the white wonders of winter.

Class Project: In Our Own Words

Retelling a class story provides an opportunity for all students to practice writing a small-moment story. Putting the stories together in a class collection lets students see the many ways of looking at a single event. This project is especially helpful for children who struggle to think of their own small moments.

1. After writing a class "small moment" story (as with the snake story), invite students to tell the same story themselves. Even if what they write is very similar to the class story, they still get practice retelling a story and writing in this form.

2. Invite children to illustrate their stories, then put them together to make a class collection of stories about the same small moment. Encourage children to notice the different ways they each told the story. Discuss their beginnings and endings. HIghlight the importance of word choice by noticing different words students chose to tell about the same thing. Take a look at the details they included: which seemed most important? Most specific?

3. Start a list of small moments that occur throughout an ordinary day. Encourage children to refer to the list if they are stuck for ideas.

Teaching Real-Life Writing to Young Learners

Name: _____ Date: _____

More Real-Life Writing Lessons

In addition to the topics featured in the preceding lessons, there are many more examples of real-life writing to enliven your writing program. Following is a quick look at a few of these. Use these ideas as inspiration for Writing Center activities, as topics for mini-lessons, or as the beginning of a more in-depth lesson. For more ideas, invite children to suggest examples of writing in their lives. You're sure to come up with some new reasons to write!

Creating Business Cards

Every child is an expert at something! Business cards are a fun way to let them share this with others.

1. Show children an example of a business card, or several different cards. Ask them what they notice about the cards. Make a list together.

   Business cards include:

   ❖ Name

   ❖ Job or position

   ❖ Phone number

   ❖ E-mail address

   ❖ Mailing address

   ❖ Sometimes a picture

2. Explain that many adults have business cards to share with other people. Usually business cards tell what someone's job is and how people can contact them (such as a phone number, e-mail address, and mailing address). Ask students to think about something that they are really good at, or a job that they do at home or school. Explain to them that today for writing, they will be designing their own business cards. Remind them of the list that you created together and that all of the information on the list needs to be on their cards.

3. Let children try out a few ideas (such as horizontal and vertical layouts) before they get ready to publish a real card on card stock. It may take a while for them to get the size of the writing correct! Practicing first will give them permission to make some mistakes and try lots of ideas before settling on one card.

Writing "About the Author" Information

Children are familiar with the About the Author information that appears in many of the books they read. This is another fun example of real-life writing for your young authors to try.

1. Share a few examples of the About the Author section from books that children are familiar with. Ask students what they notice. Make a list together.

   ❋ Tells the author's name

   ❋ Tells what other books the author has written

   ❋ Tells about awards the author has won

   ❋ Tells what the author enjoys doing (hobbies)

   ❋ Tells where the author lives and sometimes gives information about family and pets

2. Many children will notice that About the Author information "sounds a little funny," like someone else has written the paragraph. Have children look carefully at how the writing begins and point out that the paragraph begins with the author's name and that the paragraph is written about the author. They'll write their own About the Author pieces in the same way.

3. Invite children to write an About the Author piece to use for upcoming publishing parties. This can be difficult for children, but once you model this form of writing, they will catch on quickly.

Recording Observations in Science Journals

Children love to learn about bugs, creepy-crawly things, and experiments that they often think are magic. Introduce a Science Journal as a special place to record their observations and discoveries.

1. Following a science experiment, record observations on an easel as a way of modeling this form of writing. Incorporate a variety of experiments that lend themselves to a variety of charts, tables, and diagrams to provide opportunities to teach different ways of recording observations.

2. Have students use the modeled observation on the easel as support for writing in their own journals. The more you model, the more success children will have at using their Science Journals independently in future lessons.

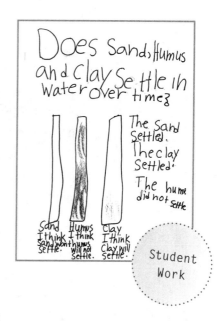

Student Work

Using Conversation Journals

There are many differences between writing letters, postcards, and quick notes. Notes are often shorter than both letters and postcards, and are an appealing form of writing for children. This Conversation Journal provides lots of practice, and is a perfect way to get to know students better at the beginning of the year and connect with them throughout the year. I usually expect students to write notes in their Conversation Journals once a week and I respond to their notes the following week. It is a great place for them to get ideas for stories and for you to ask questions such as "Who do you play with at recess?"

1. Explain that when you write a note, it is shorter than a letter. It is to tell someone something quickly. People leave notes when they will not see the other person or have time to tell the person something important. Share examples of occasions when you might write a note (for example, to let your family know that you'll be home late).

2. Explain that a Conversation Journal is a way to exchange notes between two people. It's like a conversation in writing. Their Conversation Journal will be a dialogue between themselves and you, their teacher.

3. Give each child a small journal (a 3- by 5-inch spiral notebook works well). When children open the journal, they will notice that you have written a short note to them. Their job will be to write back to you. Remind children to start their note with a greeting ("Dear _____") and end it by signing their names.

Composing E-mail

Communicating via e-mail is part of our children's future. Teaching children how to effectively use e-mail can be a difficult task. Many elementary classrooms and schools have a shortage of computers, and children may not become independent with typing skills until at least third or fourth grade. Both of these challenges make it difficult to teach e-mail writing. However, writing e-mail is a skill that can be easily modeled and taught as a whole group in the younger grades.

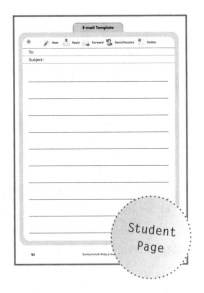

1. Begin by explaining to students that each morning when you arrive at school, you turn on your computer and check your e-mail. Ask them if they have ever used e-mail or if their families have e-mail at home. Explain that you check your e-mail to see if your principal has e-mailed any changes for the day or a parent has e-mailed to say a child will be out sick. Using e-mail is a way to send a short message without having to wait for the message to go through the mail system. It is a lot like making a phone call or leaving a message on an answering machine or in voice mail.

2. Explain to students that you will need their help today. Share an appropriate scenario for writing an e-mail, such as to ask the media specialist if a book is available. If possible, project the computer desktop onto a large screen for children to see.

3. Walk students through the steps for writing and sending the message, including filling in the "To" and "Subject" fields, writing the message, and signing the e-mail. Explain that the e-mail program on the computer automatically fills in the date and the sender's name and e-mail address. Take time to show students the difference between the format of an e-mail you send and one you receive.

4. Use the reproducible E-mail Template (page 94) to give children practice composing e-mail messages before they do so on the computer. Give each student a copy of the template. Review the different fields on the e-mail form and provide students with e-mail addresses they can fill in (such as your school e-mail address or a family member's). Have children complete the e-mail practice page as they would an actual e-mail, then if possible allow time for composing and sending the real e-mails on the computer.

Writing Recipes

Children love to cook! They can easily be introduced to the idea of writing recipes during almost any unit. Creating a class recipe book around a theme is a great way for children to look closely at what is involved in writing recipes.

1. Choose a unit of study and incorporate recipes and cooking into the unit. When first introducing recipes, show several examples and ask children to help you make a list of the different components, including:

   ❊ Title

   ❊ Ingredients

   ❊ Number of servings

   ❊ Directions

   ❊ Oven temperature

   ❊ Length of cooking time

2. Encourage families to work with their children to copy a recipe from home for a class cookbook centered around a specific theme or unit of study, such as Fall Harvest or Family Traditions. Make copies of the cookbook for each child to take home.

Writing Book Reviews

As a real-life form of writing, book reviews offer very practical applications for the classroom. Used as a form of response to literature, book reviews encourage children to analyze and evaluate what they've read and share that information with their peers—motivating further reading and promoting an atmosphere of active thinkers and learners.

Student Page

1. Share book reviews (of children's titles) from newspapers and magazines, bookstore flyers, Web sites (such as Reading Rainbow reviews; pbskids.org/readingrainbow/), and other sources. Point out that people have jobs reviewing books. Discuss how book reviews help people make choices about which books to read and even buy.

2. After sharing several book reviews, have children talk with partners about common features they notice. Bring the class back together to share ideas. Create a list of features that book reviews include, for example:

   ❇ The book title and author

   ❇ A summary

   ❇ What the author does best

   ❇ The type of illustrations (for example, collage), quality of illustrations, and how well they match the text

   ❇ Other books by the author or illustrator that readers might want to know about

   ❇ A recommendation ("If you liked the book . . . you won't want to miss this one.")

3. Revisit a recent read-aloud, and model how to use the reproducible Book Review Form (page 95) to write a book review.

4. Stock the Writing Center with copies of the Book Review Form and invite students to use them to critique books they read. Offer opportunities for students to publish their reviews, such as in a binder, on a wall display, or at the library.

Teaching Tip

As children become comfortable with writing book reviews, take time for a mini-lesson on leads. Lively character descriptions and memorable quotes from a text are just a couple of interesting ways to begin a book review. Children can use leads as a starting point for moving away from a more formatted approach (as with the reproducible Book Review form) to one that invites more of their own voice.

Conducting Surveys

Children are naturally curious about the world around them, making surveys a natural real-life writing form to incorporate in the classroom on a regular basis. Surveys are fun for students to create and offer endless opportunities to practice math skills such as data collection and analysis, and to form connections between subject areas (math, science, social studies, and literacy).

1. Surveys are conducted on almost every imaginable topic in person, by phone and mail, on the Web, and through e-mail. Share examples of published surveys. As is possible, choose those that relate to children's lives—for example, surveys about books, pets, hobbies, and favorite snacks. Identify features of surveys, including survey questions and types of responses (such as open-ended and closed).

2. Discuss reasons for surveys. Ask: "How do surveys help people? What do people learn when they ask, for example, about kids' favorite snacks?"

3. Use the reproducible Favorite Snacks Survey (page 96) to model how to conduct a survey. Begin by brainstorming healthy snacks and listing five on the survey form. Then complete the survey with a group of 10 volunteers. Show students how to record responses using tally marks and how to record a tally total for each favorite snack.

4. Have students work with partners to conduct the same survey. Make arrangements in advance to survey groups of students in neighboring classes. This will eliminate overlap and allow children to gather information from a larger pool.

5. Invite students to share their survey findings. Encourage discussion about the similarities and differences in the survey results. Ask questions such as:

   ❋ What did this survey tell you?

   ❋ What surprised you about this survey?

   ❋ Why do you think the survey results might be the same? Different? What does this have to do with the people you interviewed?

   ❋ Who do you think would be interested in using information from this survey? Why?

   ❋ How do you think the results would be the same (different) if you surveyed more people? People of a different age or grade?

Teaching Tip

Work with students to graph survey results. Publish their surveys and results in appropriate places, such as the cafeteria or school newsletter. Have students use the Favorite Snacks Survey as a model for creating new surveys on topics of interest to kids. (See also the reproducible Classroom Survey, page 46.)

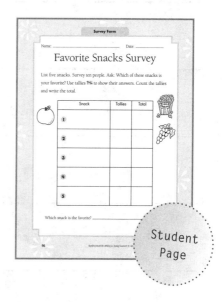

Student Page

E-mail Template

New   Reply   Forward   Send/Receive   Delete

To:

Subject:

_____

_____

_____

_____

_____

_____

_____

_____

Teaching Real-Life Writing to Young Learners © 2010 by Paula Jensvold. Scholastic Teaching Resources

Name: _____ Date: _____

Star Book Review

Title: _____

Author: _____

Type of Book:

_____ Fiction   _____ Nonfiction

_____ Mystery   _____ Poetry

_____ Fairy Tale   _____ Other

Summary:
This is a book about _____

_____.

The Writing:
I give the writing in this book ☆ ☆ ☆ ☆ ☆ stars.

Here's why: _____

_____

The Illustrations:
I give the illustrations in this book ☆ ☆ ☆ ☆ ☆ stars.

Here's why: _____

_____

My Opinion:
Read this book if _____.

Name: _____ Date: _____

Favorite Snacks Survey

List five snacks. Survey ten people. Ask: Which of these snacks is your favorite? Use tallies ⟊⟊ to show their answers. Count the tallies and write the total.

Snack	Tallies	Total
1		
2		
3		
4		
5		

Which snack is the favorite? _____

Teaching Real-Life Writing to Young Learners © 2010 by Paula Jensvold. Scholastic Teaching Resources